"Devora Zack knows networking, and her mission to make it easy and fun for you comes through on every page."

—**David Bach, #1** *New York Times* **bestselling author of** *The Automatic Millionaire*

"Let's face it, you have to network. Devora Zack's innovative strategy enables the networking-averse to succeed and have a great time doing it."

—**Joe Thomas, Dean, Johnson Graduate School of Management, Cornell University**

"No, you don't have to run around collecting a business card from every single person at every single meeting. Devora Zack proves you can make lots of new connections that will help you professionally and personally and still be true to who you are."

—**Jeff Weirens, Principal, Deloitte Consulting LLP**

"I highly recommend this lighthearted, eminently practical book by a type-A introvert. (No, that's not a typo!) It's like having a trusted friend there at each step of the way as you become a world-class networker."

—**Jeff Martin, Vice President, Human Resources, CSC, Inc.**

"Reading this incredibly enjoyable book is the next best thing to having Devora whispering in your ear, coaching you through events, and then leaving when you need time to yourself! You'll gain perspective, confidence, and the willingness to take risks."

—**Peter Borden, Vice President, Sapient Corporation**

"You are going to love reading this book! Devora Zack connects with the reader like no other business author I have ever read."

— **P. J. Kuyper, President, Motion Picture Licensing Corporation**

"What fun joining Devora as she explores the battlefield of business networking. If you've got a reception in your future, grab this book in advance!"

—**David Mayhood, President, The Mayhood Company**

"This brilliantly written, eminently practical guide *really* works. Read it today!"

—**David Meisegeier, Technical Director, ICF Consulting**

"Devora shines a refreshing new light on what it means to be a stellar networker. Focusing on quality and sincerity rather than quantity and triviality, she teaches us how to make solid, lasting relationships."

—**Kye Breisath, former program analyst, U.S. Office of Personnel Management, Presidential Management Fellows Program**

networking for people who hate networking

Who looks outside, Dreams.

Who looks inside, Awakens.

—Carl Jung

DEVORA ZACK

networking for people who hate networking

A FIELD GUIDE
FOR INTROVERTS,
THE OVERWHELMED,
AND THE UNDERCONNECTED

Berrett–Koehler Publishers, Inc.
San Francisco
a BK Life book

Berrett-Koehler Publishers, Inc.
235 Montgomery Street, Suite 650
San Francisco, CA 94104-2916
Tel: (415) 288-0260   Fax: (415) 362-2512   www.bkconnection.com

ORDERING INFORMATION

Quantity sales. Special discounts are available on quantity purchases by corporations, associations, and others. For details, contact the "Special Sales Department" at the Berrett-Koehler address above. Individual sales. Berrett-Koehler publications are available through most bookstores. They can also be ordered directly from Berrett-Koehler: Tel: (800) 929-2929; Fax: (802) 864-7626; www.bkconnection.com

Orders for college textbook/course adoption use. Please contact Berrett-Koehler: Tel: (800) 929-2929; Fax: (802) 864-7626.

Orders by U.S. trade bookstores and wholesalers. Please contact Ingram Publisher Services, Tel: (800) 509-4887; Fax: (800) 838-1149; E-mail: customer.service@ingrampublisherservices.com; or visit www.ingrampublisherservices.com/Ordering for details about electronic ordering.

Berrett-Koehler and the BK logo are registered trademarks of Berrett-Koehler Publishers, Inc.

Printed in the United States of America

Berrett-Koehler books are printed on long-lasting acid-free paper. When it is available, we choose paper that has been manufactured by environmentally responsible processes. These may include using trees grown in sustainable forests, incorporating recycled paper, minimizing chlorine in bleaching, or recycling the energy produced at the paper mill.

Library of Congress Cataloging-in-Publication Data

Zack, Devora.
    Networking for people who hate networking : a field guide for
introverts, the overwhelmed, and the underconnected / Devora Zack.
— 1st ed.
        p.   cm.
    Includes bibliographical references and index.
    ISBN 978-1-60509-522-6 (alk. paper)
    1. Business networks.   I. Title.
    HD69.S8.Z34   2010
    650.1'3—dc22   2010022238
                                                    CIP

First Edition
15 14 13 12 11   10 9 8 7 6 5 4 3

Designed and produced by Seventeenth Street Studios
Illustrations by Jeevan Sivasubramaniam and Jeremy Sullivan
Copy editing by Kristi Hein
Cover design by Susan Malikowski. Cover photography by Jan Will and Ben Goode, 123RF.

. . . for my guys.*

contents

this book is required reading

Only connect.

—E. M. Forster, *Howards End*

Learning Latin in Greek

On my first day of grad school at Cornell University, I attended micro-economics. The professor, in an attempt to calm our first-year jitters, explained in soothing tones that he would be showing a lot of graphs, yet there was no need to panic. He said, "Just think of graphs as flow-charts, and you'll be fine." As an arts professional with no background whatsoever in economics, I suddenly felt dizzy as my vision blurred. I had never heard of a flowchart. I was doomed.

I later described the experience of those first few weeks in business school as like trying to learn Latin in Greek . . . except I didn't know Greek either. No matter how earnestly I took notes, a few hours later I had no idea what they meant.

A comparable pitfall exists when a self-declared *non-networker* tries very hard to follow networking rules written for a different species altogether. There is no point of reference. No mental bucket exists in which to dump the data. The data is fine. It is just in a foreign language. *This* networking book, on the other hand, is written in language spoken and understood by introverts, the overwhelmed, and the underconnected. What luck! You finally have a chance at a passing grade.

By the way, I now return to Cornell annually—teaching MBA students networking skills. I have yet to be asked back to lecture on economics, however.

Networking for People Who Hate Networking.

Why would such a book exist? Isn't it a bit like giving quiche recipes to people allergic to eggs and cheese? Or surrounding oneself with fragrant flowers despite suffering from severe hay fever? If you have an aversion to something that is not absolutely necessary, why not find something else to occupy your life? Why torture yourself?

These are solid questions. Thanks for asking.

Allow me to begin by saying I agree with you 100 percent. Do not waste a single precious hour on an activity you hate! Still, you are not off the hook that easily. You do not get to place this book back on the shelf (or e-shelf, as the case may be), proclaiming yourself oil to networking's vinegar.

Instead, I am going to perform the astounding trick of making networking an enjoyable, rewarding activity. All without mind-altering substances! So find a comfy chair or patch of grass, crease this spine, and commit. You won't regret it.

This field guide begins by politely examining—and then shattering to pieces—traditional networking truisms. Commandments along the lines of:

- Promote yourself constantly.
- More contacts = higher probability of success.
- Never eat alone.
- Create non-stop touch points.
- Get *out there* as much as possible.

Until today (reality is subjective), networking books have been written for people of a particular temperament—the very personality style that is already predisposed to enjoy the prospect of spearing cheese in a room full of bustling strangers.

We will discover early in the book that this personality type comprises a paltry 30 to 50 percent of the general population. I am certain this is an unintended oversight on the part of other, well-meaning authors. Nevertheless, smoke comes out of my ears just thinking about it. The other 50 to 70 percent of humankind are being ignored. Misled. Bamboozled. It is time for the rest of us to take back our rightful share of the networking world.

And along the way we will discover the enormous value of understanding and leveraging our natural style when networking. No more stamping out our instincts.

Why Bother?

What's that you're mumbling? You don't like networking and have no interest, anyway? It drains you? It never works? You don't have time? You don't need to? It's phony, self-serving, fake, inauthentic, superficial, conniving, manipulative, and useless?

Hold it right there. Take a sip of water. Pull yourself together.

Introverts, the overwhelmed, and the underconnected fail at traditional networking by following advice never intended for us in the first place.

In my experience, people who proclaim to hate networking also believe they are not good at it. In fact, the reverse is true. You have the raw materials to be a stellar networker. You are simply following the wrong rules. Standard networking advice fails you, so you assume you fail at networking. Plus you *hate* it.

Now, at long last, you can learn a method of networking in keeping with the true you. Not a moment too soon.

What Is at Stake?

Only whatever you most want to accomplish in your life. No biggie.

Networking allows you to achieve your potential. Think of a Big Goal. Perhaps you want to find a new job, achieve a promotion, make a new professional or personal contact, improve the world, expand your influence, sell a product or service, write a book, seal a deal, improve collaboration, build a reputation, achieve your dream, or grow a business?

Networking will further your aim. In fifteen years as an executive coach, I have never met a person who did not benefit tremendously from learning how to network—on his or her own terms.

What is networking, really? Networking is the art of building and maintaining connections for shared positive outcomes.

Real networking is connecting.

The more authentic you are, the more resilient and valuable networks you create. You can learn networking techniques that rely on being true to yourself, using strengths you already have. You can learn to work with, rather than fight against, your lovable introverted, overwhelmed, and/or underconnected self. Previously labeled liabilities are now your finest strengths.

Enticed?

Return on Investment (ROI)

Time is your most valuable asset (unless, perhaps, you are fabulously wealthy). What about this field guide merits devoting a couple hours of your precious time to it rather than *all* the other competing options out there?

a. You will learn a new, super-effective method of networking described in accessible, easy-to-understand language.
b. You will gain dozens of practical tips while learning clear, relevant action steps with *direct* application to your own networking goals.
c. You will benefit from reading and investigating a myriad of memorable, real-life examples from my many years in many fields.

Grab a pen or pencil; you'll need it. There is no such thing as a free ride. Glad to have you along.

CHAPTER ONE

welcome to your field guide

Trust yourself. Then you will know how to live.

—Johann Wolfgang von Goethe

People swear up and down that I'm an extrovert.

This drives me nuts! I deny these accusations adamantly and then am subjected to a laundry list of supposed examples as to why I am mistaken. "But you give seminars for a living! You give presentations to huge groups and seem to love it! Plus, you know how to work a room..."

Blah, blah, blah.

These people have no idea what it really means to be an introvert. Plus, they assume that being an introvert *by definition* implies that one cannot be a strong speaker or networker.

Together, we will dispute, disprove, and knock upside the head these assumptions.

Welcome to your indispensible networking field guide for introverts, the overwhelmed, and the underconnected.

Your Author and Tour Guide

As we embark through the uncharted terrain of networking for people who hate networking, you want to be certain you are in capable hands. Why am I qualified to lead you on this journey?

First of all, despite protests from well-intentioned, ill-advised naysayers, I am an off-the-chart introvert. I am also nearly always overwhelmed and decidedly underconnected. My idea of a good time is being all alone. I have conversations with people in my head that I think actually took place. I need time to process ideas thoroughly before responding—or I get myself into trouble. The idea of a free-floating happy hour propels me into free-floating anxiety. A cacophony of external stimuli doesn't excite me; it drives me away. I easily and naturally pick up on nonverbal cues many others miss. I prefer a few deep relationships to a large group of friends.

None of these preferences is linked to my exceptionally high energy level, propensity for public speaking, or business success. That's because these attributes are not related to what defines introversion, a topic I have researched and taught about extensively for over fifteen years.

I am Type A, and I move fast. These traits are also not related to introversion.

Let's have some fun. I will present examples of attributes that, to the untrained eye, may seem extrovert-centric, but with a bit of analysis emerge as introvert-friendly.

My favorite sport is running.

Even some "experts" claim that introverts are for some reason slower and less active than extroverts. This is baloney. Think about running—a fundamentally solitary sport that requires a singular focus for extended periods. The runner can think without interruption for the whole length of the run. What a perfect fit for an introvert!

I give two to three presentations weekly.

Whoa! This statistic combats most introvert stereotypes head on. Although I am a private person, I make a point of telling clients I am an introvert (on behalf of introverts everywhere). Introverts are entirely capable of being skilled public speakers. In fact, introverts prefer clearly defined roles and so may be more comfortable leading a discussion than participating in one. Many introverts are more at ease in front of a group than roaming aimlessly through a cocktail party.

I love networking.

Herein lies the book's focus. This was not always the case for me. I discovered some wonderful techniques that turned the world of net-working upside down—or shall I say right side up? You, too, can gain insights that allow you to excel at and enjoy networking. You can be a networking superstar.

Seem impossible? I am here to tell you it is not.

A Brief History of the Introvert

Many readers of this book are introverts. Many have been taught through cultural cues that introversion is a problem, a deficit, something unfortunate to hide or overcome.

From a young age, introverts receive the message that it is an extrovert's world. *Go play with others. Join in on the game. Class participation is part of your grade.* Kids who withdraw around crowds are labeled as anti-social rather than applauded for being self-regulating.

Introversion is innate, and preferences are observable early on. As a kid, I asked for games to play by myself—a request that could prompt some parents to conduct a thorough psychological examination. As a parent now myself, I recognized clear traits indicating an introverted preference in one of my sons from the age of three.

THE BIG THREE

Introverts are *reflective, focused*, and *self-reliant.* These characteristics lead to the following key distinctions between introverts and extroverts:

Introverts think to talk.	Extroverts talk to think.
Reflective	Verbal
Introverts go deep.	Extroverts go wide.
Focused	Expansive
Introverts energize alone.	Extroverts energize with others.
Self-reliant	Social

Why not indulge yourself and use all three characteristics at once? Take some time to ponder these traits (*reflective*), in depth (*focus*), while alone (*self-reliant*). I'll wait here.

Regardless of temperament, by linking your strengths to customized techniques, you will be well-positioned to network away. Introverts, extroverts, and *centroverts* (definition ahead!) can all benefit from this field guide.

Did I mention that I am psychic? I sense you are curious where you land in all this. Right this way . . .

CHAPTER TWO

assess yourself

We do not see the world as it is. We see the world as we are.

—Anais Nin

Reverse-It Quiz

1. Why do extroverts have voicemail?

2. Why do introverts have voicemail?

Answer:

1. To never miss a call.
2. To never answer the phone.

Identical actions can spring from divergent motivations. This point reminds us there is more to behavior than meets the eye.

I am often told the observation of action is *proof* of another's motivation. This is never true. Inferences reveal only the observer's bias. The reasons *behind* behaviors reveal intentions.

MENTAL ELASTICITY

Physical flexibility requires pliable muscles. Maintaining and building dexterity necessitates an ongoing commitment.

Mental flexibility means having customized responses to people and events and also requires continual development. Mental agility requires the ability to adapt without much lead time.

Conveniently, our pals the neuroscientists (always there when needed) have a name for this phenomenon: *elasticity*. Mental elasticity can be learned and developed. This term describes the ability to be flexible in our approach to situations. Thinking in new ways builds elasticity.

From creative problem solving to crossword puzzles, anything that stretches the mind contributes to the development of a healthy, flexible mindset. Elasticity keeps brains young and prepared to meet challenges with fast, innovative responses.

Understanding dimensions of yourself through assessments also increases the brain's elasticity. And gaining clarity about your preferences allows you to better develop all aspects of yourself. Self-knowledge naturally flows into a better understanding and acceptance of differences in others. Perceiving differences is at least as important as identifying similarities.

Do not compare your insides with other people's outsides.

Negative judgment often stems from an error in comparison— using one's own internal state to critique another person's behavior. My need to work uninterrupted may clash with your need to break up tasks with frequent, spontaneous conversations. Understanding different styles takes a relationship further than making critical, erroneous assumptions.

Each number presents two statements. Assign 3 points between each pair, based on your point of view. Point distributions are 3 and 0 or 2 and 1, no half-points. If you relate to A and not to B, A = 3 and B = 0. If you agree a bit with A but more with B, A= 1 and B = 2. Respond based on your nature, not what you think is "right."

1.	A	Brainstorming is best when ideas are spontaneously shared.
	B	Brainstorming is best when topics are distributed in advance.
2.	A	An ideal day off includes time on my own.
	B	An ideal day off is spent with others.
3.	A	People may consider me to be a private person.
	B	People may think I talk too much.
4.	A	When networking, I am good at circulating the room.
	B	When networking, I usually focus on one or two people.
5.	A	I prefer working independently.
	B	I prefer working as part of a team.
6.	A	Ideas come to me by thinking things over.
	B	Ideas come to me by talking things through.
7.	A	I prefer being with a group of people at lunch.
	B	I prefer one-on-one or alone time at lunch.
8.	A	I am uncomfortable making small talk.
	B	I am a natural conversationalist.
9.	A	I make friends wherever I go.
	B	I have a few true friends.
10.	A	I often feel misunderstood.
	B	I am easily understood.
11.	A	I have numerous, diverse interests.
	B	I have a few interests I pursue in depth.
12.	A	Colleagues get to know me easily.
	B	Most colleagues do not know me well

Now enter your points and total the columns.

Assessment Scorecard

1.	A =	B =
2.	B =	A =
3.	B =	A =
4.	A =	B =
5.	B =	A =
6.	B =	A =
7.	A =	B =
8.	B =	A =
9.	A =	B =
10.	B =	A =
11.	A =	B =
12.	A =	B =
Totals	Extrovert =	Introvert =

31–36: Strong preference for your dominant style

25–30: Preference for your dominant style

19–24: Slight preference for your dominant style

So, how did you do?

There are no better or worse results. It is not possible to fail this assessment!

Strength of Preference

Let's begin with a quick lesson in personality assessments.

Anyone with half a brain realizes there are more than two types of people. To contrast introversion and extroversion (I/E) does not imply that all extroverts—or all introverts—are just like everyone else in their category. Although I/E is a significant component of interpersonal style, many additional factors contribute to one's overall personality. Furthermore, *strength of preference*, as identified on this assessment, impacts how strongly a person identifies with defining traits for each type.

People who score 25 or higher on extroversion are said to have *typed out*, to use my nerdy personality assessment lingo, as *strong* or *clear* extroverts. These people exhibit—or at least identify with—many extrovert characteristics.

The same can be said of introverts with an assessment rating of 25 to 36.

A person with a total higher score of 19 to 24 (for either column) is in the category that I dub *centroverts*. Particularly in the 19 to 20 range, this person could take the assessment again tomorrow and flip sides. A score of 18 for each, exactly in the middle, indicates neither an introvert or extrovert preference—also qualifying one for centrovert status. This happens all the time and is not cause for undue anxiety. Everyone has bits and pieces of both traits—it is just a matter of strength of preference.

Individual reactions to the questionnaire results follow three standard patterns:

1. This is me!
2. I'm in the middle . . . is that OK?
3. I knew this wouldn't work.

Let's examine these responses in more detail.

1. "This is me!" is a typical reaction when assessment results confirm one's own expectations and self-perception. Those with a strong preference along the I/E continuum often fall into this category. The more a person identifies with one end of the spectrum, the more she relates to the descriptions of that social style.
2. "I'm in the middle . . . is that OK?" people exhibit minor preferences and land in the center of the I/E scale. These respondents tend to be concerned by the results—"Does this mean I am wishy-washy or somehow weak?" To the contrary. Those who score mid-range have the easiest time relating to people all along the I/E spectrum. Anyone can train himself to learn to relate to different styles; it just comes most naturally for centroverts, in the middle of the continuum. Other factors—such as a high self-awareness, familiarity with self-assessments, and a strong background in communications—also contribute to the ease with which one relates to different temperaments.
3. "I knew this wouldn't work." At times, assessment results contradict a respondent's self-image, causing one to question the assessment's validity. A respondent might say, "I think I'm an

extrovert, but my results say I'm a strong introvert!" If you find yourself in this position, reflect on your mind-set while taking the assessment. Were your responses based on your inner nature or on how you tend to behave in certain challenging situations? Have you taught yourself to be flexible in situations that demand stretching yourself?

When in doubt, retake the assessment while thinking about your *preference*, not your learned ability. Keep in mind your natural, internal reactions, not what you perceive to be an ideal. Confusion may also arise from misperceptions you apply to the terms introversion and extroversion.

CAUTION: EXTREME READING CONDITIONS

A strong introvert exhibits more telling introverted traits than a slight introvert, and the same can be said of extroverts.

This book frequently focuses on those introverts and extroverts with the clearest preference, because distinctions are most easily understood when examining the strongest examples. There is some discussion of centroverts, who identify with certain traits on both sides of the spectrum. This field guide will also prove quite useful and relevant to centroverts.

Keep in mind your assessment results when reading. A higher number accompanying your I/E preference means more examples will ring true for you. Readers with slight preferences will relate with varying degrees to the examples provided.

The terms *strong* and *slight* reference the degree of identification with one's primary style. This has no relationship to whether or not someone has a strong personality, firm convictions, or can bench-press two hundred pounds.

Quantum physicists have discovered a very cool phenomenon with direct relevance to networking. Amazing. The experiment has been tested numerous times, providing validity to the fascinating findings.

Here's the scoop. Two subatomic particles are physically connected, then separated. From that point forward whenever one is impacted, the other instantaneously reacts even if hundreds of miles away. This effect is called interconnectivity. Once a connection is established, the particles retain a relationship without a physical link.

Because people are made out of atomic particles, this experiment has logical ramifications for human relationships. We can relate these scientific findings to connectivity in business and networking.

Building points of connectivity with others is a critical component of successful networking. Discovering links of commonality with others sharpens our receptivity to maintaining connections. Introverts' ability to focus and ask well-formed questions means an innate ability to forge real connections. Conversations go deeper, catapulting relationships into a new dimension.

Cultivating a couple of connections has more tangible results than dumping a slew of cards into the ol' briefcase. Introverts connect. Not with everyone or all the time, yet our natural gravitational pull is toward lasting relationships with others.

With the right attitude, a focus on your strengths, and a few tablespoons of willpower, you can become an expert networker—applying the personality you already have. Very handy.

I would be negligent if I didn't mention that connecting takes a bit more effort than holding up the wall while pretending to check your messages.

Higher risk, higher return.

Meet me at the next chapter, where we will gleefully smash to smithereens some standard, shallow stereotypes.

CHAPTER THREE

the destruction of stereotypes

Dare to be yourself.

—Andre Gide

Whaddaya Know? Quiz

True or False:

1. Introverts are shy.
2. Extroverts are outgoing.
3. Introverts can be "fixed" by learning extroverted traits.

Answer:

1. False
2. False
3. False

Labels such as *shy* and *outgoing* have no direct correlation with introversion and extroversion. There are outgoing introverts (right here!) and extroverts who identify with shyness. High-functioning introverts, centroverts, *and* extroverts all have a bulky toolbox of behaviors at their disposal . . . and nobody is being "fixed."

If you're in a hurry, peruse this handy chart provided for your exclusive use:

Introverts	Extroverts
■ Inner directed	■ Outer directed
■ Think to talk	■ Talk to think
■ Energize alone	■ Energize with others
■ Enjoy few stimuli	■ Enjoy simultaneous stimuli
■ Need concentration	■ Need diversions
■ Focus on thoughts and ideas	■ Focus on people and events
■ Prefer one-on-one discussion	■ Prefer group discussion
■ Value privacy	■ Value public sharing

Everybody else, let's take a field trip to . . .

INTROVILLE AND EXTROLAND

Unbeknownst to the general public, two divergent cultures live among us. Although not distinguishable by gender, age, race, ethnicity, physical abilities, or height, they are entirely different species. These two civilizations have some variations within their societies, yet retain distinct customs and rituals.

Those from Introville can be identified by a propensity to vanish alone and make their finest decisions while staring aimlessly out a window. They are capable of achieving depths of concentration that could cause them to miss earthquakes right at the epicenter.

Those hailing from Extroland move in packs. They freely share the majority of thoughts that enter their minds, pursue new interests regularly, and make friends at every turn in the road.

Due perhaps to plate tectonics, both species have been radically intermixed across the globe, even within close-knit families. There are no visible indicators of one's heritage! You could easily approach someone who appears to be just like you only to discover this person speaks a foreign language, has alien habits, and entirely misunderstands your intent. Concepts such as *respect, relationship,* and *recreation* are translated into vastly different terms in each culture.

To make this dynamic even more colorful, meet the centroverts. Centroverts are a sizable community originating from the border regions of Introville and Extroland—simultaneously at home in both and neither of the two aforementioned nations.

Your sole hope to manage this complex demographic phenomenon? A quality field guide. At your service.

A Crash Course in Introverts

Repeat after me: "Introversion is not pathology!" Or just write it down. No need to speak, interrupting your train of thought.

What traits does the term *introvert* bring to mind for you? My survey of thousands of people over the past several years has generated the following predominant responses:

Quiet	Shy	Insecure	Detached
Awkward	Not Team Player	Private	Secretive
Stubborn	Standoffish	Antisocial	Boring
Rude	Unfriendly	Distant	Aloof
Slow	Low energy	Spacey	Nerdy
Dull	Sedentary	Self-engrossed	Isolated
Uninteresting	Elusive	Negative	Moody

It doesn't take a rocket scientist to recognize that the majority of these descriptors are commonly perceived as negative in our society.

For years, researchers claimed 70 percent of the general U.S. population was extroverted and only 30 percent was introverted. When I was studying for my Myers-Briggs Type Indicator (MBTI) certification in 1994, these were the percentages we memorized. The statistic has since shifted significantly to nearly fifty-fifty (see Myers, McCaulley, Quenk, and Hammer, *Myers-Briggs Type Indicator Manual,* Consulting Psychologist Press, 1998).

I have a theory on this change. (Although I've not conducted a study, I am convinced I am correct—and I think you'll agree.) I believe the population has always been about 50 percent introverts. The previous disparity in numbers reflected the fact that introverts didn't respond to surveys about personality type! I envision the additional 20 percent of introverts balking at the surveyors, thinking, *Why would I share personal information with this complete stranger?* Some smart researcher along the way must have discovered a method to penetrate this barrier.

How do you spot the elusive, chameleon-like introvert? With difficulty. Overall, introverts seem to be better equipped to spot an extrovert than vice versa. I rarely encounter an introvert who is surprised to learn that a stranger who just related his life story is a citizen of Extroland.

It is much more difficult to determine with certainty that one is in the company of an Introville native. Here are observations, supplied by actual introverts, about their compatriots' revealing habits!

- She evaporates with no forwarding address, emerging refreshed.
- He takes a lot of notes, referencing them prior to speaking up.
- She sits at the far corner table during business trip breakfasts.
- He opts out of optional evening programs and events.
- Even after spending significant time with you, she still neglects to share basic facts about herself.
- He takes his time with opinions, yet has firm convictions.

This brings me to one of my favorite real-life examples. A seminar participant asked me whether personality style impacts the way colleagues greet one another at work. I then asked the group how they acknowledge others when passing in the hallway. A strong introvert replied, "I raise my eyebrows."

We all busted up laughing. How quintessential.

Happy exploring! On your journey, remember to bring patience, silence, a Polaroid, and an acute sense of humor. Introverts pop out of hiding just when you least expect it.

Through numerous activities and examples, this guide teaches the networking-hater how to tolerate, even enjoy, networking by applying three new guiding techniques. The 3-Ps are founded on the belief that quality networking is really about connecting.

Even networking-lovers will benefit. As an extrovert confided in me, "I think I'm a pretty good networker. But my best networking has always been from forming meaningful connections." So there.

Guiding Principle	Supporting Technique	Starting Foundation
Think to talk.	PAUSE	Research, absorb, strategize.
Seek depth.	PROCESS	Focus, learn, prioritize.
Energize alone.	PACE	Connect, reflect, recharge.

We will dive deeper into these astounding 3-P techniques in upcoming chapters. Unlike 3-D, no special glasses are required.

Introverts don't have to be fixed or managed.

This book stands on the premise that introverts, the overwhelmed, and the underconnected are equipped with enormous strengths. When we tap rather than cap our true nature, the sky is the limit.

Ready to explore the basics in more detail?

Introverts Think to Talk (Reflective)

This first principle addresses how we think. Introverts process the world by thinking through and even writing down their impressions, reactions, and responses. In contrast, extroverts primarily process verbally— discovering what they think through discussing thoughts live-time.

Notes From the Field

Anybody out there?

I was on the phone with a new client. We had not yet met face-to-face. I asked a question, and he paused so long I thought we had been disconnected.

I asked awkwardly, "Hello? Are you still there?"

"Yes." He struggled to explain: "It's just that my mind works faster than my words."

Ding! Ding! An introvert clue, I thought to myself.

A couple of weeks later, I told him of my internal response to his internal processing, and we laughed at this perfect example of introverts in conversation.

Introverts require time to process data before properly responding. We need to carefully think through responses; this makes us more committed to our spoken ideas than extroverts, who decide what they think as they are speaking. Introverts can reply without thinking—but these replies tend to be inaccurate or incomplete.

When an introvert bonds with another person, the introvert frequently becomes quite chatty. The other person can be an extrovert or an introvert; just as likeminded people are drawn together, opposites also attract. Think about a time you clicked with someone. Did you surprise yourself with how talkative you became? Introverts aren't necessarily shy or quiet. Our talk-o-meter rating is quite circumstantial.

Introversion is about what goes on internally, not what is observed externally.

Watching behavior provides insight; the introvert's inner motivation is hidden to all but the most gifted observer.

PAUSE

The first principle, thinking to talk, means that introverts (and many centroverts) need time to plan. Therefore, our first guiding technique is to pause before initiating interactions. Introverts do well by strategizing an approach, researching options, and clarifying goals in advance of taking action.

Introverts Go Deep (Focused)

This second principle focuses on how we are in the *world*. What is your comfort zone? Introverts are focused, so we can lose ourselves in the task at hand and pursue interests and people in depth. Introverts are highly selective in relationships, and how we spend our time.

Introverted networking requires a deeper focus on fewer individuals—a practice with high potential for lasting relationships.

When introverts are excited by a concept, they drill down. After many of my presentations, I get stormed by crowds of introverts. They do not dash out of the room like field mice. They enthusiastically proclaim that understanding these concepts enables them to understand themselves—and others—in a revised, more positive light.

Introverts don't do well with interruptions because we nearly always delve into tasks—it is jolting and disorienting to be unceremoniously pulled away. A stream of interruptions frustrates us and reduces our effectiveness.

Here's a play-by-play. Say you're an introvert. You concentrate on a task. You *become* the task. You enter the flow of the cosmos. An extrovert whizzes over to you, cheerfully asking whether you want to join a group heading out for, well, anything. You decline. And then you can't quite pick up where you left off. It's over. Bye-bye, flow.

A corollary to this principle is that introverts can be intensely private. Whereas extroverts freely share a plethora of personal data, introverts tend to keep quiet about their lives and accomplishments. Innocuous inquiries from extroverts are interpreted as personal, probing, and even rude.

PROCESS

Introverts and centroverts strive for, and crave, depth in relationships and experience. Rather than flitting around at a conference, draining limited, precious resources by engaging with every Tom, Dick, and Harry, people who traditionally hate networking do best by focusing on a few individuals.

A major benefit of processing a situation prior to diving in is that less energy is expended for better results. I know this works firsthand. When I attended the largest conference in my field, hoping to find a prospective publisher, I did my research in advance. I narrowed my target down to one (one!) publisher and had a single meeting at the conference. And here we are.

Introverts Energize Alone (Self-Reliant)

The third principle is linked to the self; specifically, how we obtain and maintain energy. Introverts are *inner-directed*. This means introverts renew their energy alone or with a close companion.

Strong introverts crave alone time (*I-time*) as if it were oxygen in the lungs for survival. I can become short of breath from inadequate alone time. *I-time* is non-negotiable for a high-functioning introvert. Without *I-time,* an introvert can suffer from distraction, imbalance, exhaustion, and irritability. Reserves run dry.

Honoring—rather than ignoring—this need allows introverts to direct their attention to social demands such as networking with exceptional results.

PACE

The best technique to manage this third, sparkling principle of networking is to pace yourself. This is not just a good idea—it is mandatory for anyone who has claimed to hate networking in the past. This phase is best described as a two-step continual loop. Create meaningful, real connections. Retreat to recharge. Repeat.

Teamwork

Sometimes I separate introverts and extroverts before assigning each group a task. The introverts do not begin by speaking together. Heads bend toward the table as they pick up pens to begin individual lists. Frequently, after a moment they ask, "Do we need to do this as a team?" I say yes. They then create a list that clearly states individual ideas and contributions.

The extroverts bond rapidly into a group. They are the first to volunteer to share their findings, by proclaiming, "We'll go!" They shout out over each other. No one cares. They don't check in with each other regarding their responses. No one is offended.

Often the introverts don't offer to share their list when the extroverts are finished. When an introvert does volunteer, she will begin by checking in with the group members verbally or visually to ensure no one minds if she shares their discussion points. Her raised hand is not accompanied by calling out.

Her list is short and precise, yet she provides additional details when presenting. She clarifies and elaborates. Each contribution is explained, yet not attributed to specific people. That information is deemed personal.

This composite example draws on hundreds of programs in which I have seen astonishingly consistent results.

While we hover near the topic, I want to dispel once and for all the misnomer that introverts are not good team players. It is time to put this unseemly rumor to rest. Naïve people (please lend this book to them whenever possible) subscribe to the faulty logic that because introverts are inner-directed they do not play well with others. Introverts can be exemplary team contributors by applying their attributes of focus, attention to detail, and the ability to see beyond the surface.

I will concede one point—to prove that I am reasonable. Once on a team, an introvert prefers a discrete task and the autonomy to carry it out.

A FEW BENEFITS OF INTROVERSION

- Strong sense of observation → attuned to subtle non-verbals
- Innately independent → think for themselves
- Focus on internal over external → do not notice or care much about externalities

- Heightened need for privacy → extroverts can perceive relationships with introverts as one-way
- Difficulty handling interruptions → networking requires adapting to mercurial conversations
- Drained by small talk → simple banter can wipe out an introvert's energy reserve

A Crash Course in Extroverts

At first glance, extroverts seem to be naturally adept networkers. When I teach courses on *Networking for Extroverts and Introverts,* the introverts respond with shock that any extrovert would ever voluntarily attend such a seminar. Don't the extroverts have it all wrapped up?

Yet voluntary enrollment hovers at fifty-fifty.

The class divides by temperament, and we go from there. It turns out the extroverts have plenty to learn—from introverts!—about networking. What a shocker. Once we pass around the smelling salts to revive the faint of heart, we proceed.

In these seminars, stereotypes are crushed. It turns out even extroverts have networking challenges.

A solid chunk of the people you meet—and network with—are primary extroverts. So pull yourself together, put on your field gear, pick up your pen, and (if you're not an extrovert yourself) set out to understand this mysterious culture.

Take Action!
"The Other Half"

Let's dispel the myth of the extrovert. Jot down your uncensored judgments and perceptions about extroverts:

_____	_____
_____	_____
_____	_____
_____	_____
_____	_____

Add additional reams of paper as needed. It's good to get this off your chest.

In some of my seminars, introverts and extroverts collaborate on a list of stereotypical perceptions of extroverts at work. Ready for this slam?

Noisy	Brash	Egocentric	Loudmouth
Show-off	Confident	Manipulative	Excessive
Self-promoter	Inappropriate	Talkative	Attention grabber
Intrusive	Smoothie	Schmoozer	Gregarious
Annoying	In your face	Clueless	Superficial
Shallow	Fake	Nosey	Chatterbox
Cliquey	Self-engrossed	Poor listener	Selfish

Just the people with whom you want to hang out, right?

This list provides examples of how extroverts can be perceived, yet none of the judgments are empirically true. As in "two is greater than one" true.

We get this intellectually. We do not, however, always function from our intellect. To quote the charming band the Lemonheads, "It slipped my mind that I could use my brain." (The Lemonheads, "Rudderless," *It's a Shame About Ray*. Atlantic Records, 1992.)

Well put.

Remember the handy chart linking introverts' defining traits to their preferred networking style? Extroverts merit their own chart.

Guiding Principle	Supporting Technique	Starting Foundation
Talk to think.	PATTER	Discuss, verbalize, chat.
Seek breadth.	PROMOTE	Expand, join in, broaden.
Energize with others.	PARTY	Socialize, interact, engage.

Later in the book we will artfully lace and layer the two preferred styles together, like a couple of well matched French braids. Good things come to those who wait. For now, we will trek deeper into extrovert territory.

Extroverts Talk to Think (Verbal)

Extroverts are verbally inclined. Herein lies a distinction between these two adjoining territories. Let me be clear—extroverts *talk* to *think*. This is so fundamentally disparate from the introvert's core that it leads to a plethora of differences.

Extroverts may express opinions they discount moments later. Speaking enables extroverts to work through ideas. This is a major departure from what goes on in Introville. It is the source of much aggravation and angst among introverts, who are known to carefully weigh their words before utterance.

Extroverts slide into networking mode with ease. Because they verbalize so naturally, chatting comes easily to them. They almost always prefer discussion to silence.

I take yoga classes populated by introverts and extroverts. Classes end with a relaxing closer, designed to leave participants centered and balanced—reenergized. So the introverts tiptoe around, not wanting to break the glorious silence. And the extroverts? The moment the new age music is switched off, they burst into lively conversation, "Wasn't that wonderful? I feel fabulous!"

Each time that occurs, I am reminded of how extroverts express a surge of energy. Words bubble forth.

Extroverts are Expansive

While introverts delve deeply into projects and relationships, extroverts gravitate to a range of experiences and interests. Extroverts cast a wide net, whereas introverts focus in on fewer topics, interests, and people.

Extroverts are likely to exhibit a sincere interest in many subjects—however briefly. This tendency serves them well in networking circles when meeting a range of people. Variety is the spice of life.

Extroverts enjoy environments with diverse stimuli, activities, and options. More is more. An introvert's cacophony is an extrovert's symphony.

PROMOTE

Extroverts jump right in, nearly always up for trying a new experience, group, conversation, or event. Extroverts welcome the opportunity to expand their network, with quantity trumping depth of connection. While broadening their professional or social network (extroverts are comfortable with plenty of overlap here), promoting themselves is a natural fit.

A sincere interest, even drive, to get involved in a range of activities conveniently provides a diverse platform for selling their services.

Extroverts Energize with Others (Social)

Extroverts gain energy from socializing. I'll say it one more time! Extroverts are *energized* by casual conversation. For the standard introvert, drained by small talk, this is a difficult concept to grasp. Yet this same trait can also be the source of some envy, when we introverts are honest with ourselves.

Extroverts in my seminars have been known to proclaim, "I can talk to anyone about anything!'" Introverts stare with mouths dropped open, as if upon their first viewing of a UFO.

PARTY

Extreme extroverts interact on the assumption that social interaction —of any quality or length, at virtually any time—is preferable to silence.

For strong extroverts, mingling is a relaxing, rewarding aspect of work. I have heard innumerable extroverts make proclamations along the lines of "Networking is the easiest part of what I do." Extroverts engage strangers in conversation with ease. Many extroverts consider social functions a highlight of their jobs. Party on!

A FEW BENEFITS OF EXTROVERSION

- Spontaneous interactions → engage in conversation with little effort
- Comfort in a range of situations → at ease with diverse people and circumstances
- Release of grudges or slights → easily let go of conflict, do not take things personally

HAZARDS OF EXTROVERSION

- Poor follow-up → prefer in-the-moment to closing-the-loop
- Provide a plethora of information → a tendency to ramble or provide unnecessary details
- Freely share private information → a lower bar for what is considered personal*

CHEAT SHEET!

Introverts	Extroverts
Think to talk	Talk to think
Go deep	Go wide
Energize alone	Energize with others
Reflective	Verbal
Focused	Expansive
Self-reliant	Social

Networking Preferences

Listening	Speaking
Calm	Activity
One-on-one	Groups

Networking Strategies

Introverts/Centroverts	Extroverts
1. Pause (Research)	1. Patter (Discuss)
2. Process (Focus)	2. Promote (Sell)
3. Pace (Restore)	3. Party (Socialize)

---

*I can't resist sharing this exchange with you. An extrovert reviewed this summary of hazards and protested, "What's wrong with openly sharing private information? Why is that a hazard?" In the spirit of free speech, her opinion must be heard. Extroverts! Discuss both sides of the issue during your next schmooze break.

CHAPTER FOUR

why we hate to network

Be kind. For everyone you know is fighting a great battle.

—Philo of Alexandria

Grrrr . . . Quiz

1. Why do you *really* hate networking?
   a. It is a waste of time, without value.
   b. It's in your blood.
   c. You are incapable, and that's that.

Answer:

b. Literally! And in your genes. Read on . . .

Saber-Toothed Tigers and You

You enter a networking event. You arrive a half-hour after it has begun. You walk into the large room and are bombarded with sounds and activity from all sides. Your heart rate increases, your pulse speeds up, and adrenaline races through your veins. (Is that all the same thing? You get the idea.) Imperceptible beads of perspiration form.

You involuntarily glance at your watch, although you arrived just a moment before. Why did you come to this event? You must have had a logical reason, but it is fading fast. You *hate* this stuff and don't want to subject yourself to this superficial baloney. To think that instead of being here you could be relaxing alone somewhere, even reading a book.

You vaguely recall a stress management, self-hypnosis seminar you attended in college, part of your mid-term procrastination strategy. The facilitator said to breathe deeply when under stress. What annoying advice. If she were here right now you'd tell her what you thought of her breathing.

Okay, hold it right there, buddy.

Let's take a trip down memory lane—way before your college experience. To the days of the saber-toothed tigers and cave people. Our environment has changed enormously since then, but human physiology hasn't altered all that much. When a person perceived himself to be in danger, he really was in a life-threatening situation. The physical response was to jolt into the *fight-or-flight* state. His body prepared to either run like crazy and get the heck out of there or fight like his life itself depended on it . . . which it probably did.

We humans are stuck in the past.

Fast-forward to the networking event in question. Your mind identifies the situation as threatening, and your body reacts to the perceived danger as if a saber-toothed tiger might leap through the wall at any moment. Although today this is rarely the case, our physiological responses still kick in with the fight-or-flight response.

Most of your blood flows to your extremities to prepare for battle or a long run. Where does all that extra blood come from? A great question! Your brain. Your mind donates blood to your arms and legs. This exodus of blood from your head leaves you unable to think very clearly. So when someone approaches you asking a question about yourself, your response comes out muddled; you are a shadow of your potentially vivacious self.

I hate to tell you this, but that old adage about taking a few deep breaths is valid. When stress causes our physiology to direct blood to the extremities, our breathing becomes shallow, not entirely filling the lungs. Sometimes we even hold our breath without realizing it.

Drawing oxygen down to the diaphragm (below the rib cage) improves blood flow. Deep, even breathing causes—guess what? A relaxation response. Panic subsides, blood flow increases to the brain, and your thoughts clarify.

Before presentations I find a quiet spot. At times a bathroom stall is as swanky as it gets. I will breathe deeply a few times to ensure clear thinking and increased receptivity. It works, it's fast, it's portable, it's legal across the globe, and it's free. It doesn't get much better than that.

Notes From the Field
A Peek Behind the Curtain

My work in theater taught me a lot about life and communication. For starters, the communication that goes on inside our own heads.

Think back on the last time you watched a film, play, or TV show and thought, "That's great acting!" Now think of another time you thought, "These actors stink! So fake!" If you do not have professional theater experience, how did you know whether you were watching good or bad acting? Just a feeling?

A major factor contributing to quality acting is what goes on inside the actor's head. A lousy actor memorizes lines and speaks them aloud. The result is a flat, phony performance because there is nothing substantive going on inside. The character has no supporting thoughts. There really is no character, merely an actor reciting words.

A serious actor, supported by a gifted director, sits down with the script and determines for every sentence spoken, even for times when he is standing on stage and not speaking, what is going on inside the character's head. This is called the *subtext*. The text is the script, what we hear spoken. The subtext often differs dramatically from the text. The audience may never know what it is; we are merely left with a sense of believable complexity and depth of character. A line may be, "Pass the pepper," while the character is thinking "I am madly in love with you!" The silent depth behind the dialogue changes everything.

The sum of the subtext is the *inner monologue*—the ongoing loop of thoughts that bring a character to life.

Life is like that, in reverse. We ordinary folks also have an inner monologue going in our heads and subtext for the words we utter. The inner monologue happens automatically. It is virtually impossible to eliminate unless one is highly skilled at meditation. When we sleep our subtext transforms into the dream state. In another book we can explore the value of deciphering dreams.

Yet learning to control our self-talk (civilian lingo for subtext) forms the foundation for how we interpret and respond to others. In networking, our inner thoughts inevitably affect our outward success.

CATASTROPHIC THINKING

Catastrophic thinking is one of my favorite psychological disorders, and a modern twist on the saber-tooth threat. An event occurs. Rather than thinking, "That event occurred!" you instead head into the dynamic, exciting journey of catastrophic thinking. Temporary setbacks transform into full-scale disasters, leaving you overwhelmed, in a heap.

Reframing

Whether you love, tolerate, or hate networking is directly correlated to your inner monologue. It is never too late to rewire your brain! All you need is a small set of pliers and a solid dose of willpower.

Throughout this book I reference the term *reframing*. Like many of my beloved concepts, it is elegantly simple. Imagine you have a picture in a black frame that's nothing special. One day you reframe it, selecting a perfectly customized frame, accentuating the picture's colors. The whole picture appears improved, not just the frame.

This concept provides the foundation of reframing. We frame experiences based on our perceptions and past experience. Taking a moment to place a new frame on objective reality can dramatically change our understanding of events and people. Altering our perception enables a change in response and behavior. Reframing is a particularly handy concept for overwhelmed, underconnected non-networkers.

Do you think you are a good networker? If not, why not? Many people associate networking with working a room; approaching strangers, making chit-chat, and freely divulging personal information.

What if we reframe networking as an opportunity to create meaningful connections, requiring skills such as listening, focus, and depth? Do you think you have these abilities? Does this change your visceral response to the concept of networking?

SELF-TALK

Do you beat yourself up with self-talk reinforcing a belief that you aren't interesting, worthy, or confident? What endless audio loop do you run through your consciousness daily?

Self-talk is how we speak to ourselves within our own heads. Everyone has different self-talk patterns, styles, and habits.

From years of exploring the facets of self-talk, I have identified themes. Some self-talk patterns place a negative veneer on events; others emphasize the positive. Here is a summary of these styles.

Negative Self-Talk	Positive Self-Talk
■ Emotive	■ Reflective
■ Exaggerated	■ Realistic
■ Limiting	■ Expansive
■ Discouraging	■ Encouraging
■ Catastrophic	■ Manageable
■ Victim	■ Learner
■ Grim outlook	■ Good humor

Let's dispel the myth that negative self-talk is somehow more honest than positive self-talk. Positive self-talk is more realistic. Negative self-talk exaggerates the impact of what occurred:

It was a disaster! I blew it and will never recover. I will never go to a networking event again.

Positive self-talk tells it like it is:

You know what? I am looking to make a career change, so I went to an industry event. It's true: I dripped spinach dip down the front of my white shirt shortly after walking in. I accidentally introduced myself using the other person's name at one point because I was looking at his name tag and was distracted. But I crossed the hurdle of getting out there, and everyone spills sometimes. Next time I go to an event, I will eat beforehand.

Negative self-talk attributes blame, whereas positive self-talk requires taking responsibility for whatever the situation presents.

Positive self-talk replaces a victim's perspective with a learner's approach.

How could this happen? ⟶ **What can I learn?**

Take a breather from reading. Try this technique.

Take Action!
"Self Image and Networking"

Recall a recent situation during which you engaged in negative self-talk. Write the actual event or sequence of events in the left column. In the middle column list any negative thoughts you had during and immediately following the event.

Now imagine alternative, supportive responses. Write these in the "Revised, Supportive Self-Talk" column. Envision the impact of implementing this upgraded version of reactions.

Event(s)	My Perceptions and Negative Self-Talk	Revised, Supportive Self-Talk

Here is a sample completed form, based on the previous *botched-networking-event-with-spinach-dip* example.

Event(s)	My Perceptions and Negative Self-Talk	Revised, Supportive Self-Talk
I am looking for a career change, so I signed up for a networking event with some influential people. I was late. I came straight from work and promptly dripped spinach dip down my shirt front. Then I introduced myself to an industry leader using his name. I took his card to end the conversation and left soon after.	They have to schedule construction during rush hour, making me half an hour late to this darn event that I shelled out forty bucks to attend. I was famished. Like a complete idiot, I start shoveling in this green dip to take the edge off my hunger, and wouldn't you know it? Spill it all over my white shirt. Embarrassed and distracted, I am approached by this bigwig sticking his hand out; I look at his nametag and I introduce myself as him. This guy couldn't believe how stupid I am, I could see it in his eyes. When I asked for his card, he probably wished he didn't have one.	I am proud of myself for taking a concrete step toward a career change. I hit traffic, but plenty of people arrived after me. I spilled dip on my shirt, but got most of it off with a napkin and it was hardly visible behind my tie. It was great that the guy who arranged the event made a point of introducing himself to me, and we both got a laugh out of my faux pas when I said his name for my own. I'm sure he'll remember me, and I can make a humorous reference to it when I thank him in an email tomorrow morning.

WARNING LABEL!

Revising habits is tough, and negative self-talk is sticky. It is harder to scrub away unwanted habits than to scrape price-tag residue off newly purchased glassware.

Tips are in order.

1. The brain can't *not do* something; it can only do something. Ask a neuroscientist—there must be one around here somewhere. If not, just take my advice. It is futile to think *I shouldn't think those thoughts*, because you can't *not* do something. You've probably heard the "Don't envision a pink elephant" illustration. If not, never mind. Focus here. When you have negative self-talk, simply replace it with a revised, positive version.

2. Rather than attempt to cease all limiting thoughts, start by increasing your awareness. Making self-talk conscious is an important step.

3. Resist the urge to have negative self-talk about your negative self-talk, if you catch my drift. Negative self-talk is normal and reversible.

It is worth the trouble. Improving self-talk requires virtually no time investment, as it is all contained in that gorgeous head of yours. Positive self-talk improves your perspective, attitude, and mood. All this combines to convey a more positive, confident self-image.

CHAPTER FIVE

sparkling new rules that work

The summit of happiness is reached when a person is ready to be what he is.

—Desiderius Erasmus

"It Happens to the Best of Us" Quiz

True or False:
Drained introverts can be a tad touchy.

Answer:

True. There is no point sugarcoating the reality of the matter.
Learn how to network without becoming overwhelmed
and exhausted. You will *feel* better and *do* better.

If you consider yourself overwhelmed or unconnected, there is a good chance you attempted to network in the past, and have since decided you'd rather schedule a root-canal than attend your next mandatory business event.

Standard networking advice is extrovert-centric and fails most introverts and centroverts. Many of these folks proceed to interpret this disconnect as their own shortcoming. "If *that* is how to network successfully, then I am a networking train wreck." I've lost track of how many introverts have informed me, with deep conviction, "I am a terrible networker." As if this conviction is an indisputable fact and there's nothing we mortals can do about it.

Typical advice isn't inherently flawed; it's just geared to a subgroup of the population. Let's say I lived in Miami and wrote a book on how to locate palm trees. "Go outside, walk around a while, and you'll come across one soon enough," I would write, and it would be solid advice in Florida. Yet a devotee of my writing in Boise may walk around for a couple of days and reach the conclusion he isn't cut out to discover palm trees. Eventually he may realize the book simply wasn't written for him.

My sparkling new rules are custom-designed for people who hate networking. I've discovered this group encompasses a cross-section of introverts, centroverts, and even extroverts. A bonus of these rules is that they also serve those who already love networking, teaching them how to better relate to those with different styles.

Rewrite the Rules

Typical tips are not particularly useful for networking-haters. We do not succeed by denying our natural temperaments; we succeed by working with our strengths.

Why does the same advice that makes extroverts giddy sink like a rock in the stomach of introverts? Experiences that fill an extrovert with glee make an introvert feel inauthentic and exhausted.

Go ask an extrovert for networking tips. You'll find one nearby, chatting with the others. His recommendations may include acquiring lots of contacts, meeting as many people as possible, and filling your calendar with events.

An introvert who foolishly attempts to follow the string of advice blithely offered by a gifted extroverted networker will collapse faster than a soufflé at a fireworks display.

Follow your energy. If you turn every meal into a networking opportunity, you will drop from exhaustion within two weeks. There is nothing wrong with eating alone regularly. It can be the highlight of your day and a vital component of your networking success. Solo time is how many people process data and revive energy.

A drained introvert is an ineffective introvert.

What is really going on is I am a bad extrovert. Similar to *I am bad at writing with my right-hand* when I am left-handed. Sure, I could learn, but why go against my natural style? Why don't I instead focus on being a gifted left-hander?

I love to eat lunch alone. So much so that every week, throughout my freshman year in college, my mother would phone to ask if I had eaten lunch with anyone. And because the answer was generally no, she fretted for a year that I had no friends. That was not the case, and when she reads this book she can finally breathe a sigh of relief, twenty-five years later.

Some things don't change. Now as a consultant and coach, my solo meals perusing a magazine are an oasis of calm to reenergize. I eat about nine out of ten meals alone. When I do have lunch (or breakfast or dinner) meetings, I am totally on. What happens when I schedule daily lunch meetings? Production goes down, I am wiped out, and the meetings are ineffective.

Connecting versus Collecting

Successful networking requires that you be true to yourself. You are the foundation from which to build. Attempting to transform yourself into another type of person is a dangerous business that will leave you dazed, confused, and plain old wiped-out. I cannot condone such reckless behavior.

Why not revel in who you are? Doesn't that sound a lot more fun, relaxing, and validating? Success starts with being real. If you are overwhelmed, try to start enjoying the ride instead of dwelling on what you *should* do. *Should* is not very inspiring. (You should never say should.) If you are underconnected, revisit your definition of that term. If you are an introvert, that is fantastic; you are well positioned to win all kinds of networker-of-the-year awards. Start jotting notes now for your acceptance speech.

Introverted and extroverted networking boils down to a basic distinction:

Extroverts collect. Introverts connect.

If you're an introvert, you may have unpleasant memories of standing at a corporate event like a wilting networking wallflower, wistfully watching extroverts swirl around the room collecting—people, business cards, and toothpicks from those tasty hors d'oeuvre platters. Perhaps this observation convinced you of your own inadequacy: *I don't want to talk to these people, and they don't want to talk to me. I'm outta here.*

The old rules are not inherently bad, they are just limited. They work—for the approximately 30 percent of the population that identify as strong extroverts. The centroverts (20 percent of moderate/slight extroverts + 20 percent of moderate/slight introverts) and introverts do not directly benefit from the old rules. Our sparkly new rules, on the other hand, are user-friendly for introverts, centroverts, and even plenty of card-carrying extroverts.

Let's take control of this situation. Join me in turning three old-school networking premises on their heads. Drum roll, please.

Dusty Old Rule #1: Jump On In (Patter)

There is no use beating around the bush. Let's face facts: extroverts can talk. All you introverts, stop rolling your eyes! Graciously cede the point.

Extroverts talk to think. Sometimes this habit causes boundless aggravation for introverts; other times it spurs envy. The fact is, the ability to maintain a friendly stream of patter enables extroverts to keep a conversation flowing, a discussion lively, and an event afloat. They know it, introverts know it, and we all may as well accept it.

Jumping on into situations and discussions is one way to build contacts. Extroverts are quite comfortable talking with virtual strangers—otherwise known as new friends. Extroverts like spending as much time as possible interacting with others. This is why a verbal person is well-positioned to take the advice of old rule #1 and run with it.

What about everyone else?

Sparkling New Rule #1: Pause!

When I ask extroverts to describe introverts' strengths, they invariably describe introverts as good listeners and planners. This compliment seems to be an undisputed win for introverts, as extroverts are equally forthcoming about their own need for development in the same areas. Not that it's a competition. (As my youngest son says, "It's not a race, but I'm winning.")

Understanding that I, as an introvert, think to talk enables me to turn a potential shortcoming into a skill. In my consulting and coaching practices I dedicate plenty of planning time before meetings to review strategies and think through responses. Implementing the first new networking rule—pause—I am able to communicate with clarity and precision.

As one of my seasoned clients observed, "We learn primarily from observing, not from speaking." So if you do not have a gift for chatter, focus on what you do have—a predisposition to watch and gather data.

Notes From the Field
Silence Is Golden

I was facilitating a *Communication and Personality Style* program for high-level engineers. Mandatory attendance was decreed from above. Ninety-five percent of the attendees typed out as introverts and centroverts. My questions met with silence. We flew through the agenda.

Fortunately, I knew better than to interpret this behavior as negative, disinterested, or off-putting. I am comfortable with the silence that introverts require to process, and the attendees' nonverbal cues indicated their full engagement in the course content.

This belief was confirmed at our first class break. I was bombarded with students asking one-on-one questions. By lunchtime, I could hardly break free to get something to eat; introvert and centrovert members of the group were adamant about talking over concepts introduced and delving deeper into course topics.

Virtually all the participant questions were posed between sessions.

Dusty Old Rule #2: Sell Yourself (Promote)

Self-promotion comes more naturally to strong extroverts than to your typical introvert. Promotion is a valid networking strategy. And great advice for someone whose natural skill set includes the gift of gab.

Actual advice I have come across in this arena includes the following:

- Be visible at all times
- Share accomplishments freely
- Always reach out to others
- Be in constant touch with contacts
- Regularly update others on your successes

Promotion is a natural corollary to the extrovert's predisposition to expand networks. In many cases, promotion extends beyond oneself into the realm of growing businesses and community organizations.

A delightful, extroverted, long-time client of mine is the executive director of a non-profit organization. When I told her the name of my upcoming book, she laughed. "How could anyone hate networking? It is my favorite part of the job. I love it! Networking is my reward for doing the rest of my work." She did note, however, that she needed to read the book to better understand the introvert and centrovert team with whom she had surrounded herself!

 ## Sparkling New Rule #2: Process!

Introverts and centroverts are often uncomfortable talking about themselves and consider many topics private. You can see the hurdle to kicking off a relationship by talking about your innumerable fine attributes. However, at peak functioning, introverts learn a tremendous amount about new acquaintances. Processing enables previous networking-haters to create deep, lasting contacts with less time on self-promotion.

Notes From the Field
Still Waters Run Deep

I met Luca while facilitating a leadership seminar for seventy senior attorneys at a luxurious lakeside resort. Dinner was served at large banquet tables, where Luca was reserved and quiet.

The second morning took place outdoors and required a good deal of prep work, so I arrived early to get going. Luca was the first participant to arrive; he was there half an hour before the program was scheduled to start. He offered to help and took on his tasks with enthusiasm.

I asked what he had done the previous evening following dinner. He self-consciously said he sat by the lake watching the water. Luca confided in an apologetic tone, "I like to sit sometimes and just look at the scenery."

He said small talk exhausts him, and he prefers spending time alone during session breaks. He explained his early appearance that morning because he ate breakfast before the others arrived to ensure time alone with his newspaper, unhindered by well-meaning colleagues joining him.

Luca, now quite chatty, went on to extrapolate that he believed he appears uninteresting to people when they first meet him. In this conversation his depth, humor, and thoughtfulness were evident. I later learned that these very qualities directly contributed to his professional success. Luca held a coveted leadership position, overseeing five other attorneys.

Following the program, Luca supplied detailed feedback, complete with reflections and recommendations.

Luca exemplifies the characteristics of a strong introvert. He excels in one-on-one situations. He readily opens up when he perceives a safe situation. His richness is hidden from plain view, making its discovery that much more satisfying. He thinks to talk, and he writes with unusual clarity. Like many introverts, he has hidden layers. We are rewarded when we allow introverts to unfold on their own terms.

THE QUESTION OF QUESTIONS

If you are an introvert, make the most of your fabulous talents. Most introverts are more comfortable asking questions than revealing personal information. Tap into your high level of focus, combine deep listening with well-formed questions, and you need never again be at a loss for conversation. Furthermore, your astute attention to subtle verbal, and non-verbal (such as eye contact and full attention) information provides communication cues that allow you to gather a tremendous amount of data about others while networking.

Closed-ended questions require only a yes or no response. Open-ended questions maximize information. Consider replacing "Do you like your work?" with "What do you like most about your work?" Also, *why* tends to put the responder on the defensive. Whenever possible, replace *why* with *how* or *what*. Consider replacing "Why did you leave your job?" with "What led you to make a career change?"

Thoughtful questions build rapport. Reflect on a time you met someone and walked away with a positive impression. Most likely, she demonstrated an interest in you. Actively listening demonstrates an interest in others—a slam-dunk to making a good impression yourself.

I overheard the following description of a colleague: "She is reserved, but has a great deal of depth within her." I noticed the but. As if it is contradictory for a reserved person to have depth. I have noticed that people who initially seem reserved eventually reveal intriguing backgrounds, talents, and personalities.

Dusty Old Rule #3:
Maximize Time with Others (Party)

This advice plays directly into the first precondition for a visa to Extroland: be social. Extroverts revive their energy by spending lots of time with lots of people on a regular basis.

In a conversation with an extrovert, I was surprised to hear her say she enjoyed taking day trips alone. When I asked for details, she responded, "Sure. I just get on the tour bus and spend the rest of the day chatting with whomever happens to be seated next to me. It's great!"

Joining groups, associations, and teams enables extroverts to revitalize their spirits. Holing oneself up in a hotel room on a business trip, for example, is counterintuitive and counterproductive for someone who gets an energy infusion from being with others.

Extroverts thrive in environments with plenty of people and action.

Fill your day, your life, your time with people and events galore. There are many variations on this beloved theme of Extroland. Join the club. Ultimate success and true happiness are yours through lots of social interaction. The more the merrier. Party on.

 ## Sparkling New Rule #3: Pace!

Introverts and centroverts do best when engaged in authentic conversation, structured activity, and purposeful action. Pacing these activities allows us time to recharge. Wham! We become networking dynamos.

GIVE YOURSELF A TIME-OUT!

The dreaded penalty for the unruly three-year-old is a sweet melody to the overwhelmed, exhausted networker. You are in a time-out! Remember: *Introverts. Energize. Alone.*

We crave being alone. We require *I-time* to function. It is as basic as that. Introverts revel in this assertion from philosopher Martin Buber:

Solitude is the place of purification.

Successful networking requires both acknowledging your strengths and honoring your needs. To maintain your enviable self-reliance requires regular escapes to refuel.

What a relief. Advice that doesn't make you want to turn on your heels and head for the hills. Plus, it works better for introverts and centroverts than standard, extro-centric advice.

LESS IS MORE

High-functioning introverts replace quantity with quality. Filling life with a plethora of activities and people snuffs an introvert's flame right out.

Fewer people + Less time = Better outcomes

This equation tasks introverts with meeting one person per event, not ten. It also requires follow-up.

Quantity is an exhausting and inauthentic measurement of success for introverts.

Sure, an introvert could put the pedal to the metal and tough it out. She could dutifully follow the standard advice and devote all spare moments to networking. The results? Unsatisfying. The introvert? Panting for air.

Because introverts go deep, attempting many simultaneous pursuits can feel overwhelming. The same principle applies to pursuing many networking contacts at once. Extroverts can comfortably acquire a wide range of associates, and they are equally fine keeping superficial ties with most. This is unacceptable to introverts, who prefer maintaining fewer, more meaningful connections.

A solid, compact network of reliable contacts is the best-case scenario for the introvert.

I was the lead presenter at a three-day conference. My highly interactive sessions required enormous focus and energy. The conference was a great success, with uniformly positive feedback. However, I failed to pace myself between sessions; instead, I was constantly dashing from event to obligation and back again.

A couple of weeks later, I was surprised by the phone call I received from my client. She said a participant had told her she believed that I thought I was above it all. The participant said that when she had approached me to talk after a session—an encounter I didn't recall—I "blew her off." My client knew me well enough to interpret the misunderstanding, but I definitely appreciated getting the information.

The interaction, I was told, had taken place after the concluding program on the final day. I remember I was wiped out and prepared to dash to the privacy of my suite. I can imagine conveying a nearly complete lack of presence at that point. In my mind I was already out the door.

What I learned, and offer as advice to introverted presenters, is this: protect your I-time—yet when you are still in the limelight, maintain your presence of mind along with your presence. An unintended offense can become impossible to undo later. Pacing is not an optional luxury—it is a necessary component of a successful strategy.

An extrovert described herself to me by saying, "I'm a joiner." Precisely the opposite of how I would describe myself—and we got along great. Increased understanding leads to increased appreciation of our own opposites.

In the chapters ahead, we will apply the concepts of *pause, process,* and *pace* to diverse networking situations—including (coming right up) networking events, job searches, business trips, and running your own events.

CHAPTER SIX

networking event survival kit

Fortune helps those who dare.

—Virgil

"Hey You, Wake Up!" Quiz

1. Is *Networking for People Who Hate Networking* an oxymoron?

2. Do extroverts have networking all wrapped up?

3. Can extroverts and introverts peacefully co-exist alongside a chocolate fondue fountain?

Answer:

1. No.
2. No.
3. Yes.

Networking events are those special times in life when people gather together, generally in large numbers, to chit-chat, exchange contact info, and eat unhealthful, unidentifiable fried food in unnatural quantities.

How is a networking-hater to survive, let alone thrive, in this situation?

When I go to an event, it is *always* because I coerced myself. I am generally pleased with the results, yet I head there under duress.

It is like early morning exercise. I've been going to the gym early mornings for twenty years. I trick myself—perhaps a clue that I'm not so bright. I tell myself things like, *I'll just go to the gym to take a shower today*. Once there, I rally. The next morning the cycle starts all over again. As I resentfully bash the snooze button, I curse myself. I vow I'll never work out again—after this morning. Afterward? I feel like a million bucks.

Don't wait until you are all psyched to go networking. If you wait until the mood strikes, prepare to wait forever. You've got to kick yourself out that door. Once there, armed with your secret pause, process, pace strategy, you'll do just fine.

No wimps.

Dragging Yourself Out There

There's a big corporate event tonight. Attendance is not required, yet you are expected to go. The change of clothes you brought from home hangs from a hook on your office door. Everytime someone comes in or goes out, the garment bag swings, drawing your attention back to the event looming near the end of an exhausting week.

By six o'clock your mind is buzzing from the collective sensory bombardment of the day's events. Discussions, strategic planning, a noisy lunchroom, miscellaneous meetings, spontaneous hallway exchanges, a presentation, and a conference call have left you wiped out. You want to decompress. Your mind scans a gamut of excuses, hoping to discover a legitimate reason to bow out. Realizing it is hopeless, you put on your evening clothes and trudge to the event.

Entering the networking venue, you see unknown people milling about with nametags already peeling off of business suit lapels. The volume is high, and the mood seems cheerful—in direct contrast to your own state. People are drinking, laughing, and perusing tapas platters. You wonder how much more time is required to fulfill your obligation to attend.

An initial search for officemates proves futile. You seek out a quiet corner to check your voice messages, although you last checked them five minutes ago. Another tedious night of networking—or the failure to do so—begins.

How about a do-over? Take two.

 Pause

Preregister. This early commitment serves four purposes:

1. Gain time for mental preparation.
2. Score a preprinted nametag.
3. Reduce the likelihood of backing out at the last minute.
4. Ensure yourself a spot at important events.

I don't think I'd go to any networking events if I didn't preregister. In the moment, after a typical day of presenting, facilitating meetings, and executive coaching, the last thing I want to do is go to a networking event. But once I commit myself, I don't back down.

Plan your attire. This means more than simply dressing sharp. Appearances matter. However, this is also the time to weigh the benefits of fashion versus the value of comfort. Will that hip scarf flailing about become a distraction? Do your feet hurt after fifteen minutes of standing in designer shoes? Do your contact lenses dry out at the end of a long day, making eyeglasses the wiser choice? Does that snappy new tie not really match your suit?

It is more important to look put-together than to wear expensive clothes that don't quite work for you. Reflect on what image you want to convey. I am surprised by the overly casual attire I see at business events. Dress up a notch. Planning your clothing line-up is particularly important if you look young and want to convey a confident, professional image. Plus, you reduce game-day stress by preparing these external details in advance.

Have a quiet lunch. Enjoy a relaxed lunch perhaps reading or listening to your favorite music. Find a place where you can eat peacefully.

Stop working a little early. Create a half-hour cushion for alone time between work and the evening event. Even fifteen minutes is better than nothing.

Volunteer whenever possible. Arrange in advance to help out. Many networking-haters are most comfortable when in a designated, structured role. Working the event provides you with a specific reason to engage with others, rather than poking around for small talk.

Go with a pal. Finding a networking ally can transform your experience. I went to an event with a networking-averse colleague, and we had a blast. We challenged each other throughout the event to target others and took turns venturing out and reporting back. Our positive attitude and humor also attracted others to us. Both of us made solid connections at that event.

Clarify goals. Why are you attending? Set clear, measurable outcomes such as meeting one or two new people. Be realistic.

Arrive early. If you are hesitant to attend an event at all, why get there first? Because it is better to enter a room with a few people than one with a crowd packed close together. Gatherings are cozier near the beginning. Arriving early also presents an opportunity to help out.

Take a moment. I always regret delving right in. Taking a moment to center internally and refresh externally inevitably improves my outcome. Go to a place with a mirror—the best-case scenario is a well-appointed powder room, the worst case is a small mirror you carry in your briefcase or bag for this purpose. Check yourself out. Everyone else will; why not start with *numero uno*? Make sure you are at your best, or at least not entirely disheveled. Finish up with a few nice deep breaths.

Once, to my dismay, I discovered I was wearing two entirely different earrings. Apparently in the morning I was testing out which looked better with my outfit and experienced an ill-timed lapse of memory. I have heard others confide similarly alarming revelations about mismatched shoes, uncombed hair, and so on. These confidants will remain nameless, for now.

Freshen your breath—it can't hurt. If you decide to brush your teeth, it's better to do so prior to arrival. Leaning over a sink with a foaming mouth is not the ideal way to meet a potential new client, colleague, or employer.

 Process

Check out the nametag table. I like to spend my first moments at networking events scanning the nametags of other attendees. An early arrival ensures that most nametags have not yet been picked up, allowing me to check for attendance of those I know or want to meet. It also provides a few moments of *I-time* before crowds ensue.

Linger by the crudités. Hanging out by the food is a good standby, particularly if you skipped dinner (but don't arrive starving, then succumb to inhaling everything within reach). Food stations offer a temporary place and purpose. As others arrive, many one-liners are at your disposal, such as:

- Nice selection! (Only if there are more than two food groups.)
- Do you know what type of cheese this is? (Best if you are not pointing to cheddar.)
- Where do they get such great strawberries this time of year? (Assuming there are strawberries and it is not June.)

Food is the ultimate networking visual aid. Just take small enough bites to be able to respond to others without a five-minute time lapse for chewing. And choking is a major faux pas.

Notes From the Field

Three Cards

Following a networking event, an introverted client excitedly reported back to me that she had collected three cards. To an extrovert, this is a pittance. Yet she remembered the conversations and sent friendly, specific follow-ups: business materials accompanied by personal notes such as "I enjoyed our conversation about your recent, inspiring professional successes . . ."

She extended offers to meet for coffee; two accepted. A year later she remained in touch with both and did business with one.

Scan the room. Position yourself somewhere between the outskirts and the inner circles to obtain a good view of the maximum number of attendees. No mathematical formulas are necessary. Conduct a slow visual scan of the room. Look for those you know and those who, for whatever reason, seem approachable to you. See how gently you are being eased into actual human contact?

Talk to staff. I am referring not only to the people responsible for running the event. I mean the bartenders, coat room attendees, and anyone else working the venue. Especially those passing around large, heavy appetizer platters. It is good form to acknowledge and thank people around you, and it gives you something to do. Also, tip well. An open bar does not necessarily cover tips.

Get in line. Lines provide a fine alternative to standing around alone. Conversation openers with fellow line-mates include asking about work, origin of an interesting name, or what brought them to the event. Completing your time in the line provides a built-in closer—exchange contact information and be on your way.

Make eye contact. Most people are lousy at eye contact. Good eye contact conveys an interest in others while increasing their positive perceptions of you. Eye contact also disciplines you to stay focused on the other person rather than unrelated thoughts or negative self-talk.

Be an open target. Make yourself approachable. Consciously maintain a pleasant expression. Standing-only tables are magnets for solitary folks open to conversation. Find an open table where you can hang out with a plate or drink, or join another solo, asking whether he minds company.

Note the unusual. Notable accessories or unique styles invite conversation. People tend to purchase and wear distinct items to make a statement. You can't go wrong complimenting and inquiring about these items. I take this strategy with me everywhere I go, far beyond networking events—into meetings, elevators, and the street. It never backfires.

 Pace

Focus on others. To many, interacting with strangers is one of the least appealing aspects of networking. The most common reason being *I have no idea what to talk about!* Get this—you don't have to! People appreciate thoughtful questions. Plus, displaying an outward interest makes others like you more. Jackpot! Here are some sample openers:

- What kind of work do you do? What do you like best about your company?
- What interesting projects are you working on?
- How was your day?
- Do you have plans for [this weekend, vacations, the summer]?
- Do you want to join me in checking out the appetizers?

Focus on you. Offer a few tidbits about yourself. Socially confident introverts can artfully direct all conversation away from their carefully guarded selves; however, this can be picked up on and misread by others. People notice and become uncomfortable with one-way conversations, potentially segueing into imbalanced relationships. Others may perceive you as distant, uninteresting, aloof, or elusive. Decide in advance what you are comfortable sharing with others.

Focus away from you. Remind yourself that only you know how long you linger at the side of the room, how many times you visit the snack spread, or how many people you manage to make contact with in the course of an evening. The room is not focused on you. No one is keeping track—unless you do something supremely embarrassing. We won't dwell on this counter-productive thought.

Schedule recharge breaks. Socializing depletes an introvert's energy reserves. Sensory overload makes energy vanish faster than an open lane on the Santa Monica highway. Head out for a breather, step away to refresh, decompress on a brisk walk, or check messages.

Mitigate sensory overload. Recognize it, prepare for it, manage it. Particularly at major multi-faceted events, there can be many rooms and a lot going on. Limit yourself. Take a walk around to get the lay of the land. Hydrate to keep clear. Let go of what you *should* do.

Visit the information table. Event organizers often display information about products or services. Perusing pamphlets allows you to learn about your hosts, provides conversation ideas, and gives you the opportunity to pace yourself.

Write it down. Note pertinent information on business cards of new acquaintances. Do not overestimate your future memory capacity. Include these:

- Name, with correct pronunciation hints
- Event location and date
- Personal facts (family, birthday, upcoming travel, interests . . .)
- Brief conversation summary
- Intended follow-up

Jotting notes also provides built-in time away from continual interaction.

Ending a conversation gracefully is a valuable skill. It sure beats allowing a conversation to fizzle out past its prime. You also want to avoid making others feel trapped talking with you. Be gracious. Warmth is an asset for successful closure. To get started, check out these ideas:

- May I have your card? It was great meeting you.
- I am headed over to eat/drink.
- Have you met [colleague passing by]?
- I'm going to freshen up.
- I need to make a call.

- I've enjoyed our conversation! Thank you.
- I look forward to following up.
- I promised myself I'd circulate—I better walk around.
- I'd like to get some fresh air.
- I'm going to sit down for a bit.
- [Glance at watch] Oops, I really have to go.
- I'm sure you want to talk with some others; I won't hold you up.

If you claim to be headed somewhere, *really go* (nothing like trashing your credibility immediately).

Know when to split. Set a reasonable predetermined *sayonara* time. Sorry, ten minutes post-arrival doesn't qualify. Tune in to your biorhythms (if you don't know what these are, flip through a 1970s self-improvement book).

Watch for signs of hitting a personal wall. Refrain from judging how you *should* feel; leave before you burn out. Departing before you are drained dissipates tension for upcoming events. Fortunately, networking events don't require you to clock out, and others don't notice when you go. Follow your well-honed intuition. Leave when you have accomplished your goals—and before you feel like you're swirling around a giant drain.

Plan your escape. Have a departure plan. If you are tied into other people's schedule, find a place to wait while they finish up. You are not at your best when you overstay your capacity to be "on."

Afterward

Personalize follow-up. Introverts often excel at the written word, so writing personalized notes is an opportunity to capitalize on a natural strength. Introverts appreciate being able to reflect before committing words to paper. Specifically reference a topic from the conversation to merit a networking gold star. Ask how the new project is progressing or how coaching Jake's soccer team went. You will make a smashing second impression.

For maximum impact, go for a letter sent via actual mail. This gesture gets noticed.

Extroverts dazzle with light banter;

introverts impress with thoughtful follow-up.

If you can't manage the effort of writing a real handwritten or typed note, email is next best.

Electronic or paper, personalized notes are best when sent within forty-eight hours, while you both still recall the interaction. Memories and inspiration fade fast.

Be useful. After an encounter, consider sending your new acquaintance an article or link relevant to your conversation. Being thoughtful is better than just sending information about yourself or your business, which can be perceived as too aggressive—unless directly requested. Making this effort conveys that you remember the person and conversation and cared enough to follow up. You are also providing a service, positioning yourself as a useful person to know. This action cements what began at the event—an authentic connection. You can include your website or contact information—an opening for the recipient to learn more about what you have to offer.

Keep an up-to-date file of helpful resources. Bookmark interesting links in your browser. A ten-year-old article, unless it's an established classic, hints that you are out of touch.

Weigh the benefits and risks of email attachments. Emails accompanied by an attachment are more likely to become entangled in spam filters. If an article is short, consider including it in the body of your email. Or copy in the headline and lead paragraph, followed by the URL. If you do not hear back within two weeks, send a cheery, short check-in message. Once.

Reward yourself. Promise yourself a reward contingent on attending an event and meeting your predetermined goal. Make it as simple or special as you like, such as visiting a favorite art gallery, getting a massage, purchasing a small treat, or allowing yourself to sleep-in.

Beyond. Keep the momentum and strive beyond your comfort zone. Think about that monthly potluck your team coordinates. The one you keep missing, as you run out of feasible excuses for your continued absence. Consider joining in once, for an hour. It is remarkable what out-of-office interactions can do for professional rapport and productivity. Focus on non-work topics. Otherwise, you might just as well be at an ordinary staff meeting.

Nametags 'n' You

I spend a great deal more time than your average Joe reflecting upon minutiae such as nametags. Worse, it turns out this is a topic about which I have developed a myriad of strong opinions. Some people occupy their minds with topics as lofty as philosophy, politics, or sports scores—I am lost in the trenches of nametags. The only benefit of this preoccupation is to share with you my heavily considered insights.

Prioritize. If nametags are preprinted and your information is incorrect or misspelled, determine how important a correction is to you. To fix the information probably means replacing a prepared nametag like the ones worn by everyone else who preregistered with a handwritten version for those who were added at the last minute. If it is a misspelling of your name (Steven rather than Stephen, Michele instead of Michelle, Rebecca in place of Rebeka), you might decide to let it slide. You do not need to point out this error to everyone you meet. An incorrect title, not accurately reflecting a recent promotion, may be worth fixing.

Printing. When writing your own nametag, use the thickest marker available (i.e. a broad felt-tip, not a roller pen). Write your first name (if that is how you prefer to be addressed) in large capital letters with the minimum required additional information in smaller print below. This generally includes your last name and company name. Do not crowd your nametag with any extraneous information. If you make a mistake, throw it out and make a new nametag—do not cross something out. A messy nametag is unreadable and unprofessional.

Many people rush in and dash off their nametag without a thought. Take a moment; it becomes the most important thing you are wearing.

Pursue. Scan nametags for connectivity and points of interest. Nametags supply information you can use to initiate conversations.

Plastic. If nametags are in plastic sleeves, this is a great thing. I like to put a small supply of my own business cards behind the name card, inside the plastic sleeve. They are easily accessible, neatly in one place, and carried hands-free. You can also store business cards of others you meet during the event. Just be sure to not mix them up when handing out your own. Parenthetically, I also store my plastic hotel keys in the back of the nametag holder. There. Now you know all my little secrets.

Conversation Management

There is an endless list of questions introverts consider private that extroverts think nothing of asking a total stranger. How to respond?

Reserve judgment and try to not take offense. You don't want your friendly neighborhood extrovert taking your own boundless need for privacy personally, do you? Consider typical high-frequency questions and plan your responses. Here's a list, followed by adaptable responses.

- How long do you plan on working here?
- How much did that [fill in the blank] cost?
- What is your salary?
- Do you have a family?
- Do you like [that person]?
- How old are you?
- Who did you vote for?
- Are you religious?
- What is your opinion on [divisive current event]?
- Why do you think [that person] really got promoted?
- What do you really think of [this place/your company]?

Potential, mostly interchangeable, replies follow.

- It is hard to say. And you?
- I don't remember.
- I can't remember the last time I checked.
- Yes, what about you?
- Sure.
- Care to guess?
- I'd rather not get into that.
- It's relative.
- Depends what you mean.
- Why do you ask?
- I can't go into all that now.
- I try not to think about it.
- I'd have to think about that.
- I've not been here long enough.
- What do YOU think?

- [Shrug] Want to grab something from the buffet/bar?
- Oh, that! [Sigh.] Let's talk about something else.

A positive demeanor, light-hearted tone, and friendly smile are crucial accompaniments to all of the above. If you feel uncomfortable or backed into a corner, keep a cheery "I have to run, great meeting you," in your back pocket. Then move out of eyeshot before settling into your next conversation or breather.

Another handy trick is planning in advance what to say when you don't want to engage in conversation with someone from the start. In my case, I've noticed saying "I am a consultant" does the trick. Eyes haze over as a yawn is barely suppressed.

I am ditched in no time.

CHAPTER SEVEN

good-bye golden rule

My idea of an agreeable person is a person who agrees with me.

—Benjamin Disraeli

Making-the-Most-of-It Quiz

Why do introverts tend toward perfectionism?

Answer:

Combining an inner focus with the susceptibility for deep
pondering leads to a propensity for perfection.

The Platinum Rule

The golden rule is one of the most quoted treaties in the land of being nice to other people. There may be as many versions of the golden rule as there are languages. It can be paraphrased succinctly:

~ GOLDEN RULE ~

Treat others how you want to be treated.

Why not? Seems logical. Now let's see what really happens when the golden rule comes into play when followed to the letter.

An introvert and an extrovert are colleagues in the same department. They decide to go to a networking event together. Each believes firmly in the golden rule.

Upon arrival, the extrovert, Glen, gleefully descends on a group already gathered in the center of the room. He joins in, pulling Portia the introvert along with him. He knows she can recede in a crowd. He likes Portia and wants her to have a good time. The conversation turns to presentation mishaps, and he recalls Portia's fiasco the day before. "Hey Portia! Tell them about your hilarious faux pas yesterday!" He means well and knows the event had no lasting or important consequence. Meanwhile, Portia is inwardly mortified. The last thing she wants to do is recount to a group of complete strangers a personal, embarrassing story.

Now let's take the opposite path. Same setup, Portia and Glen at the event. Portia, as an introvert, wants to be super-sensitive to what is potentially personal in a networking situation. She is asked by a small cluster of newly met acquaintances at the event about a recent success she enjoyed at work. Although she knows Glen had a similar experience, she hesitates to bring it up in case Glen may consider that a private piece of information. Instead Glen feels dissed by Portia, not creating a natural bridge from her story to his own.

The above scenarios exemplify the Golden Rule; the colleagues are treating one another how they themselves would like to be treated. The result? Both are unhappy with the outcome.

I propose instead use of the new and improved (cue fanfare):

~ PLATINUM RULE ~
Treat others how *they* want to be treated!

I am amazed by how frequently, in even my multi-day seminars, participants cite the platinum rule as the single most valuable take-away. This concept revolutionizes interactions and communication, particularly between introverts, centroverts, and extroverts.

The platinum rule is a lot more work than the golden rule. If I use the golden rule, I get to act the same way all the time. It's easy. I just think about what I like and treat everyone else that way. Unfortunately, on the introvert-centrovert-extrovert continuum alone, I will be less than fully effective more than half the time.

To apply the platinum rule, two highly challenging skills come into play.

1. I can quickly assess, more or less, another person's natural preferences.
2. I am flexible enough to modify my own interactive style to complement others'.

Full application of the platinum rule requires adapting and modifying communication to some degree with every person you meet. One size does not fit all.

Assuming others will meet us where we are at is just not realistic. Most people are simply not that skilled to be able to apply the platinum rule well. That is why it is up to us. Yet do not despair! You do not have to get it right completely or all the time. Plus the benefits are boundless. Rapport soars and networks thrive. The effort pays off.

The platinum rule allows understanding to trump frustration. Before I understood the vast divide between Introville and Extroland, I reacted with annoyance to behaviors incongruent with my own

Notes From the Field
A World Apart

Two young men approached me during an executive development seminar to discuss a "difficult, negative" colleague. Describing Anne, they shook their heads slowly from side to side in sheer baffled exasperation. Their description of her incorrigible behavior culminated with this anecdote: "We have a birthday club so we can all celebrate together, and she refuses to tell us her birthday. She says it is none of our business!"

They paused for air, clearly expecting me to jump on the bandwagon. Instead, a realization hit me. "Wait a minute. Is this the Anne in our class?" When they responded in the affirmative, I immediately understood the situation.

I recognized that Anne was a strong introvert. Among other behaviors, I had observed her listening intently, alternating with mentally removing herself for internal processing. In the course of our two days together I had found Anne quick-witted, delightfully sincere, and notably supportive of teammates.

These two well-intentioned extroverts could not fathom why someone would rebuff an effort to join in on friendly group celebrations. Her refusal was jolting, interpreted as difficult behavior. They had stopped speaking to her altogether. Yet where Anne comes from, one's birthday is personal and private. The prospect of regular group celebrations at work seemed tedious and superficial. And being approached by colleagues for what she would define as idle conversation was a waste of time, draining, and distracting.

I did not tell them all this. It is a lot to digest. Yet I did explain how differently people can interpret events and exchanges. I recommended they neither ostracize Anne nor bully her into "having fun" according to their conception. We discussed ways to rebuild a collegial professional relationship that would work for all. Starting with a smile and nod as they passed her desk and slowly growing from there.

The follow-up status reports I received were heartening.

sensibilities. Now that I have integrated the platinum rule into my life, I respond with humor, and even gratitude, to these same differences.

Be a Sleuth. Reframe yourself as a detective, always on the lookout for clues. People bombard us with cues about how their minds work, how they function, and how they like to be treated. Tuning into verbal and nonverbal cues enables us to calibrate our communication, upping the likelihood of a positive response. You can practice fine-tuning your ability to pick up on communication clues anywhere you go. A side benefit is you never again have to be bored at a meeting or in a line. Just soak it all in.

Respect. While facilitating seminars and retreats, I notice how frequently the concept of respect comes into the group discussions. Participants implore:

- We need to respect each other more!
- She doesn't respect me.
- No one respects each other enough around here.
- It is obvious he isn't respectful to others.

What is going on around here? Are all humans inherently disrespectful? No. The problem is more fundamental—and easily solved—than that.

Respect is a vague, non-measurable concept. Respect is not easily defined. People are multi-dimensional. Even considering only the introvert-extrovert continuum, we can identify problems with the notion that respect is objective.

Let's say Rachel is out on personal leave for two weeks. An extroverted co-worker, Marissa, wishes to express respect for her acquaintance. She employs the golden rule, treating Rachel as she would want to be treated. When Rachel re-emerges in the workplace, Marissa dashes over and gives Rachel an affectionate squeeze around the shoulders. "Hey Rach! So glad you are back! I hope everything is okay! If you need to talk about anything, remember my door is always open."

How do you surmise Rachel, an introvert, is responding internally? Most likely she is feeling invaded. She does not know Marissa well. She thinks it is inappropriate for Marissa to be so chummy, and she is uncomfortable with being touched by a virtual stranger. Plus, she does not appreciate Marissa's making a scene in front of everyone.

Now an opposite scenario. Guapo, an extrovert, has also been away for two weeks on personal leave. His introverted colleague, Josh, sees Guapo return to work on Monday morning. Wanting to be respectful, Josh treats Guapo the way he himself would want to be treated. He politely says hello, yet does not behave as if there is anything unusual. Why draw attention to someone who has clearly been dealing with some personal issue?

Guapo is offended. He thinks, *How rude and insensitive of Josh! We have worked together nearly six months, I am out of the office on personal leave, and Josh behaves as if I were here yesterday. Obviously he doesn't care about anything but my productivity.*

Do you see the issue? In each case, the well-intentioned colleagues, Marissa and Josh, are employing the golden rule, treating a co-worker as they themselves would want to be treated. In both cases, their efforts backfire entirely. As a result of these earnest efforts, Rachel and Guapo are both taken aback and even offended. Each would report being disrespected.

How would the platinum rule reverse this? First, Marissa and Josh would be self-aware enough to understand their own interactive styles. They would also have to be astute observers to notice how co-workers might want to be treated. They will be wrong at times, but they make an effort. Finally, they develop the skill to flex their communication styles, so they can adapt their responses to situations and individuals.

Flexing Your Style

It is a fine line—on the one hand I say be true to who you are. On the other I say it is an important networking talent to know how to skillfully flex your style, known in the world of personality assessment as *behaving out of type*. How do we reconcile this apparent contradiction? The answer goes back to the inside and the outside.

Your internal drivers remain unchanged. You are who you are. Your behavior stems from your choices. The more aware you are, the more skilled at communication, the more astute at picking up on nonverbal cues, the more choices you have at your disposal.

A range of behaviors to draw upon increases your probability of forming real connections. I have irreplaceable, lifelong relationships with flaming extroverts. And the reason I am frequently labeled as an extrovert myself is because I can flex my own external style—and even enjoy it!

Neurotransmitter Signals and You

Neuroscientists can track neurotransmitter signals in the brain. It goes something like this. Habitual behavior occurs virtually automatically, without bothering to engage the conscious mind. Neurons fire and travel with inexplicable speed along existing neurotransmitter pathways—formed from repetition.

New behaviors, attempts at revised patterns, have no such luxury. Neurons fire without neurotransmitter signals in place. It is a much more treacherous journey. Consider entering your home through your front door. Contrast that with entering through a solid wall on the side of your home, requiring the herculean effort of smashing through to create a brand new workable entryway. This image approximates the difference in effort between an established habit and creating a new behavioral pattern.

This may seem a tad demoralizing. But wait! There is a silver lining. Taking action close to the point of inspiration instigates the ground breaking of a new neurotransmitter signal and greatly increases the probability that a new pattern will in fact be established. Writing about a fresh beginning and verbalizing it count as real first steps. Once you get a few new neurotransmitter pathways in place, flexing your style while maintaining your comfort and integrity becomes easier. Plus, the payoff from creating these miniscule pathways can be galactic.

Take Action!
"Arm Fold"

Try this experiment to make flexing your style a visceral experience. Stand up without holding anything (this is the only time I will instruct you to put down this book). Shake out your arms. Loosen up a little. Now fold your arms normally, however you would typically fold them. Hold this position for a few moments, noticing how it feels.

Shake out your arms again. Now fold your arms with the opposite arm on top. You may not wholly succeed; just do your best.

Shake out. For the third round, fold your arms normally.

Last chance to shake out—make the most of it, kick your legs, dance around a little—no one is looking. Unless you're in the library, in which case you will be encouraging a wait list for this book, which is fine with me.

For the final portion of this experiment, attempt to fold your arms with the opposite arm on top one last time.

A. Write three words or phrases to describe what it was like to fold your arms normally, the first time:

1. _____

2. _____

3. _____

B. Now select three words or phrases to describe the experience of folding your opposite arm on top the first time. Just write the first three things to come to mind:

1. _____

2. _____

3. _____

C. Was it even slightly easier to fold your opposite arm on top the second time around? Circle one response.

Yes   No   A little bit

D. If folding your opposite arm on top was crucial to your professional success and personal development, could you teach yourself to do it?

Yes   No   Maybe

ANALYSIS

This exercise is a memorable metaphor for flexing your style. When you folded your arms naturally, it was automatic—without conscious intervention. This is the equivalent of behaving within your natural personality style.

When you folded your arms with the opposite arm on top you had to consciously think about the placement of your arms and hands. This is the same as practicing new behaviors—trying out new responses to situations. When you first practice flexing your style, it feels [insert your responses to B].

Folding your opposite arm on top is easier for some people than others. An ambidextrous person may have no difficulty at all with this exercise. Similarly, a centrovert, someone who borders between introvert and extrovert, will find it relatively easy to flex his style. It does not take much effort for a centrovert to relate to or speak the same language as an extrovert. An introvert on the far end of the spectrum needs to put more effort into flexing her style.

Remember that temperament indicates one's preference, not one's ability. Another similarity between this experiment and flexing your communication style is that it gets easier. If flexing your style matters enough to you, you can learn to fold your opposite arm on top—literally and figuratively.

Notes From the Field
Flex for Success

Tanya is a highly-regarded executive vice president in a Fortune 100 company. She has remained loyal to her company, working her way steadily and comfortably up the corporate ladder. During an economic downturn, however, the company made it clear that regardless of one's role, all executives were expected to bring in business. Tanya had always been uncomfortable soliciting business and had never done so in the past. She decided to just continue her current path of high performance in her normal role.

As months passed she began to recognize the necessity of facing her reluctance to network and sell services. Did she force herself to double her social network, join in on all office socializing, start eating lunch with colleagues, and attend weekly industry events? No.

Her carefully executed strategy was a direct departure from traditional networking wisdom. She methodically reviewed her contacts, selecting a single person to approach; a graduate school friend, Mark. She spoke with Mark one-on-one and mentioned that it would mean a lot to her to arrange a meeting to discuss collaboration between their two businesses. She realized she sincerely believed Mark would also benefit from the alliance, and this conviction came across in the meeting.

Upon reporting her progress to the executive team, she was met with astonishment. It turned out that for years her company had wanted to forge a relationship with Mark's company and could never get in the door. A few months later her effort paid off far beyond any expectations. Multimillion-dollar contracts were in place, and she is certain beyond a doubt this has been her single biggest contribution to the company in twenty-three years.

As you tap into your inner networker, others will start gravitating toward you. At this point, you need to be extra aware of gauging your energy. This began for me several years ago. People responded quite positively when I embraced my introvert nature. Learning to network through your strengths is freeing. What once felt impossible, daunting, and dreadful can happen effortlessly. Others began gravitating to me in greater numbers than I could manage. It was a situation of be-careful-what-you-wish-for—as you learn to network with ease, you still need space for yourself.

Inner preferences remain the same even as outside behaviors develop, grow, and adapt.

Lots of interactions, if not carefully managed, will drain you.

I am upbeat and enjoy making people laugh. People frequently engage with me in friendly conversation. I want to be kind. Apparently, I come across as quite accessible. However, it is a bit like being on my own little reality show. Put an introvert into a world with a giant *"Talk to Me!"* sign over her head and watch what happens.

How do you advise me to handle this situation?

_____

_____

_____

_____

Good. Keep this advice in mind. As you get better and better at this stuff, you will need to remember and implement this counsel yourself.

Personality preferences are internal, not easily discernible to an external viewer. An average observer could notice an extrovert and me at the same event without picking up on fundamental differences, such as why we each came. We may have had the same motivation—to meet new people—but that is not what propelled us to show up. Maybe I came to tackle the challenge; the extrovert, because it sounded fun.

CHAPTER EIGHT

networking without a net

If there is no wind, row.

—Latin Proverb

Oops! Quiz

What type of introvert is most in danger of being labeled a snob?

Answer:

A person who exhibits confidence yet does not join in on conversations. Calibrating your energy will ensure that when you are *present* you are *on*, dissipating the likelihood of this misunderstanding.

I have good news and bad news, and it is the same news:

Life is one giant networking opportunity.

Go locate a paper bag to breathe into, re-establishing your equilibrium. Panic will get you nowhere. There is additional good news—most of life is not a networking *event*.

Networking is not an isolated situation that takes place at designated times and places. For better or worse, it is an ongoing state. At first glance, this may seem "for worse" to the average networking-avoider. You do not get to check networking off your list of things to do and crawl back under your cozy rock.

I understand that if you already consider yourself overwhelmed, this piece of news is unlikely to help matters. If you are underconnected, however, this is your lucky day. Every interaction is an opportunity. Each encounter has limitless potential. Every place you go and person you meet is a networking experience.

Not to pound this into the ground, but whenever you are not completely alone (and off-line) you are in a networking situation.

Structure Success

The overwhelmed and the underconnected can be charming networkers. Imagine you are given the opportunity to meet someone. An introductory conversation reveals the potential to mutually support one another. You exchange contact information.

- What are the chances you follow up with an email or phone call?
- How would you describe the interaction? Positive? Productive?

Those who perceive themselves to be underconnected also happen to be highly likely to follow up and maintain meaningful relationships.

Notes From the Field
The Perfect Day

In some seminars, I sort the participants into temperament teams and instruct them to write down what they would do on a perfect day. The immediate questions shouted out from the extroverts are "Can we make the list all together? Can we go on the day together?"

In many cases, they have known each other for approximately thirty seconds, and they are already fully prepared to hang out, sharing an imagined idyllic day. I say it is up to them, and they breathe a sigh of relief and immediately start brainstorming a lengthy list of events to take place on this single day, laughing and interrupting and raising the decibel level of the room.

When I ask this group which activities on their list involve other people, they boisterously reply, "All!" Their faces show me that they think this an absurd question. A day alone doesn't sound fun at all. How awful. Naturally, on their perfect day they are surrounded by *friends* (a broad term), and it generally concludes with a festive party.

The introverts nearly always present a short list of their individual, solitary pursuits. When asked what activities listed involve other people, it is their turn to laugh. The response? "None."

Centroverts—those in the middle of the I/E continuum—create their own group, and true to type, their activities are a mix of time alone and with others. A distinction is that centroverts more frequently specify who comes along (such as "my best friend") while extroverts will be more general and incorporate more people (such as "a pool party").

Pause

People who claim to hate networking prefer programs and events with a clear format and purpose.

Good choices for them? Take a class, attend professional development seminars, coordinate a brown bag event, sign up for a lecture series, join a task force, volunteer for a non-profit board, or attend an educational outing. An introverted colleague told me she will attend only structured programs, avoiding all loosely configured networking gatherings.

You are at your best when you're sincerely interested in a topic or format. When fully engaged you feel more comfortable and less self-conscious. Conversation flows more naturally.

Take Action!
"Personal Inventory"

Now is a fine time to make an inventory of circumstances in which you thrive. If not now, when? Situations that support your strengths position you for networking wins. This is a painless, affirming process.

1. Recall past experiences you enjoyed and events in which you were at your peak. Examples can be professional or personal; a range is good. Make an unfiltered list—it needn't satisfy the left side of your brain's urge to be logical or seem relevant. Take a moment, close your eyes, and take a few deep breaths to be receptive,

Previous Situation	What Made It Work	Opportunity for Success
1.		
2.		
3.		
4.		
5.		

allowing these positive memories to surface. Write up to five that came to mind in the first column.

2. Review the situations you listed. In the second column, assess what specifically about these situations caused you to feel comfortable and thrive. Examples include having a defined role, doing an enjoyable activity, intellectual stimulation, physical challenge, novel experience, inherent reward, or learning something new.

3. In the third column, brainstorm an unfiltered list of potential new situations that meet the criteria identified in column two. Here's an example of a completed row:

| I volunteered at a national professional conference in my field. | I had a defined role, enjoyed lectures, had autonomy and structure. Volunteer status made it easier to talk to others. There were opportunities to both help and learn | I could look into volunteering at a local theater, since I rarely make time to attend anymore. I will have a defined role, see the shows, and meet others while helping out. |

Notice how the original situation and the future opportunity are quite different, yet the second is modeled on what worked in the first. Also, the national conference changes location yearly, so it does not provide an ongoing networking situation. Being a regularly scheduled volunteer at a specific local venue resolves this challenge.

Being clear on your intended outcome determines the next logical step to take. If your goal is to find a new job and you want to work in the arts, the example choice is ideal. If you are an electrical engineer specializing in high-tech firms, the scenario may make sense for a different reason—if you want to reintroduce balance and the arts into your life, or you want to network outside your normal circles. If you are looking for a job in your field as the electrical engineer, perhaps your third column would read like this:

Locate a local association for electrical engineers. Volunteer for an event, and if it's a good fit, consider joining the board of directors.

Perhaps your carefully honed anti-networking predisposition is fine-tuned to protect you from inadvertently stumbling into networking opportunities against your will. This is a good time to rethink your strategy.

Not so easy for introverts, as we are a bit inclined to say no before we say yes.

What is the reason behind this phenomenon? Why are introverts likely to reject unexpected requests, changes, and challenges? Don't go getting all defensive; I notice this propensity in myself, too. I am having a good laugh right now, envisioning you stifling the urge to insist "No! That's not true!"

On a related note, I have heard the claim that introverts tend to be negative.

The reason for the stigma is because introverts need to process. When approached with a new idea, introverts without the opportunity to think it over *are* likely to simply respond with a "No." There is a way around this. When presenting a concept to a suspected introvert, don't let him respond immediately. Offer the idea, then fly out the door saying, "Let's discuss it later." You may be surprised at how receptive he has become when you return to discuss the idea a couple hours later.

Welcome to a personality behavior analyst's version of a geometrical theorem.

A. Introverts think to talk. This means we prefer to consider and weigh many angles of an idea before committing to a response.
B. If not given time to provide a considered response, the standard introvert reaction is "No."
C. If one approaches an introvert suddenly with an idea, presents it verbally, and expectantly prompts, "So what do you think?! Are

you on board?" the response is overwhelmingly likely to be negative. Thus the introvert is dubbed negative by affiliation.

If A = B and B = C then A = C.

There is no use getting agitated or taking this theorem personally. What are you to do with this exciting new insight? Accept that you may require extra time to process new ideas. Options abound.

1. Anticipate and capture "No" before it escapes your lips. Say instead that you will consider the suggestion and get back to that person.
2. Request, when appropriate, that others submit ideas to you in written form. Time to think allows an introvert to prepare and respond thoughtfully with a considered opinion.
3. When under fire, pause for a moment before verbalizing your response. Think. Silence is fine, and thoughtful replies are appreciated.

 Process

Place yourself in comfortable environments. There are certain situations that provide soothing locations to hang out, energizing the overstimulated introvert amid a hectic day. These, unlike wine-and-cheese gatherings, are indeed the introvert's natural habitat. Plus, they are teeming with introverts. We will explore three, from least to most likely to produce a network connection.

QUIET

Living near Washington, D.C., I at times ride the higher-speed Amtrak Acela train up the eastern corridor. One car on the train is designated the Quiet Car. Shortly after passengers have boarded, the conductor is fond of announcing, "If you must engage in conversation, please do so silently." I was sold immediately. Plus I get a kick out of being surrounded by fellow introverts, reveling in a train car free of cell-phone chatter, business people loudly debriefing the day, and the dings of video games. Perhaps they could put up a big sign on the car: "Introverts Only, Please!" The car is truly silent. Obviously it would be quite the indiscretion to strike up a conversation in this particular environment. However, particularly if you are a route regular, you may meet a kindred spirit.

A word of caution to extroverts. Beware of inadvertently situating yourself on this car and speaking normally. I've been amused more than once by observing a herd of irate introverts taking matters into their own hands.

SILENCE IS GOLDEN

Many public libraries have undergone beautiful renovations in recent years. Some include in their new floor plans *Silent Rooms*. These rooms generally stipulate no talking and electronics may only be operated in silent mode. Another introvert oasis. Because of the sound restrictions, they are frequently located by an exterior wall of the library, meaning windows and views. There is no supervision, so occasional whispering takes place. These little jewels are free and open for long hours. While researching this book, I attended one regularly and enjoyed the variety of people, backgrounds, and shared love of peace and quiet. Soon we were silently greeting each other warmly (a special introvert trick)—then proceeded to mind our own business. Coming and going from the *Silent Room,* regulars may strike up conversations about their work or research, so networking does spring forth.

Classes are a fine choice for introverts looking to expand their network. They fulfill the criterion of providing a defined role for the participant and are inherently valuable and stimulating. Classes can be found in virtually any topic. Plus you meet people with at least one common interest. You can choose to take classes in your professional field, supporting areas, or something entirely unrelated. While getting my MBA, I took a pottery class for stress release. This was a mistake on my part, as I learned that attempting to center clay on the wheel rivaled microeconomics on my unachievable scale. Yet my enrollment succeeded in another way: I created a lasting connection with the only other MBA student enrolled.

 Pace

You make about a billion choices each day. That is a ballpark estimate. Try to count your choices one day—including conscious and subconscious—and email me with feedback on my estimating skills. That way we won't have to speak directly.

A successful networker is adept at replacing habitual, subconscious choice with revised and improved choices. Purchase a brand-new set of choices today to get free shipping and handling.

Temperament indicates natural preference and style—without defining ability and potential. If you think to talk, adopt the strategy of planning ahead for networking opportunities. It means working with your temperament, not discounting or overriding it.

Following are choices I recommend. But suit yourself. Add, edit, delete.

1. Accept who you are.

You already have everything within you to be an incredible networker. Knowing you need time to *not* network will immeasurably boost your time spent networking.

2. Accept your reality.

Accept where you are and who you encounter. Why fight it? Who you are with is who you are supposed to be with at that moment. How do you know? What proof do you have? The fact that you happen to be currently facing or seated with that person. You can bang your fist down and fight it—or smile charmingly and make it your business to figure out why you are supposed to be talking to that person at this precise minute. How does this encounter fit into your life, on a minor or major scale?

3. Reframe failure.

Failure produces *results* that allow you to improve. Results are the means by which you measure your progress and adjust your behavior to achieve your worthy ideal.

Independent-minded introverts are not particularly focused on what others think. Introverts are not insecure; they are merely internally-driven. This is the opposite of insecure.

Contrary to urban legend, introverts are as likely as extroverts to be effervescent, exuberant, and quick-witted. At times these traits are hidden beneath a smooth exterior, exposed only when the introvert is at ease and comfortable. You gotta peel away a lot of leaves to get to the heart of an artichoke. I figure this is a better analogy than the layers of an onion, which smells and has nothing special in the middle. Work with me here.

Extroverts often express pleasant surprise at the person eventually revealed beneath an introverted colleague's protective layers. "Wow! He is really interesting," they note, following a successful retreat or other event geared to benefit professional relationships. Patience and plenty of space brings forth the rewards of an introvert's late bloom.

Notes From the Field
Promotions and You

I was coaching a vice president of an international development company who had experienced solid success. However, his career seemed to have stalled out at its present level, and after a few sessions we explored why this was the case. He revealed that he was not good at promoting himself and his accomplishments. His direct reports and close colleagues produced a string of superlatives to describe his style—to the extent that I could gather infuriatingly few areas for development.

Yet he was continually passed over for promotion opportunities. We discovered that he felt inadequate in the realm of organizational politics, and he suspected—correctly—that those in the highest leadership positions were not aware of his strengths and successes. Sure enough, when assessed he typed out as a strong introvert, and he displayed most of the expected qualities. He built lasting, strong, loyal coalitions with trusted coworkers. Yet he needed to learn to promote himself to those in senior leadership roles. Because his international company offered few opportunities for face-to-face meetings, he began sending bi-annual progress reports, always keeping this bulleted list to under a page.

At the next annual company meeting, he was determined to introduce himself to those on his short distribution list. He made personal contact, followed up with thank-you notes, and inquired occasionally about new opportunities on the horizon.

He was promoted a year later.

BE COOL

Create opportunities to make small, considerate gestures. These require virtually no time or expense and can take the place of being a chatty extrovert. Actions speak loudly. Besides establishing you as a genuinely cool person, thoughtfulness redirects your attention away from yourself toward others.

Kind gestures set you apart in the most positive way. Here are some networking examples, perfect for introverts because they take few words to initiate and can spark a conversation. These suggestions are geared to networking events but can be adapted and applied to a range of situations.

- Whenever in line for food, hand a plate to the person behind you.
- Before getting a drink or snack, ask whether anyone nearby would like something too.
- Compliment unique items (eyeglasses, tie, jewelry, and so on).
- Make a friendly inquiry about an interesting name or job title.
- Offer to provide follow-up information in areas of interest.
- Compliment special qualities (bright smile, warmth, positive energy).
- Ask about accomplishments (degrees, publications, work-life balance).
- Offer to help out (nametags, reservations, gathering materials).
- Honor preferences (standing or sitting, inside or outside).
- Make a point of introducing people you think would connect.
- Offer to pass along someone's information to others as relevant.
- Defer to the group (dining preference, timing, location).
- Inquire whether you can help break down the event upon conclusion.
- Jump in to help (spills, balancing plates, dropped items).
- Be respectful (give space, don't smoke, step away if needed).
- Maintain a calm exterior when faced with unexpected change.
- Follow through with what you offer or promise!

Introvert Alert!	Extrovert Alert!
If you want lunch one-on-one with an extrovert, make that clear! She is as likely as not to spontaneously bring someone else along.	Silence from an introvert does not convey dislike of an idea. She could be thinking it over.
Refrain from asking an extrovert a simple, yet optional, question when under deadline. You may be treated to a lengthy exposition and have no one to blame but yourself.	When faced with a quiet person, do not ask, "What's his problem?" You may be in the presence of an introvert who is focused inward and simply doesn't have anything to say at the moment.
Perhaps you have a colleague who expresses a strong opinion only to completely discount it the next day. Rather than label that person as unreliable, recognize he may have simply been speaking to discern his true opinion.	Why does your colleague stick so stubbornly to his opinions? Because introverts ponder and commit to ideas before speaking, it takes more effort to change their minds. Provide time to recalibrate before requesting a response.

MUSIC TO MY EARS

Here is an example from my own sordid past. Back in college, the first extracurricular activity I pursued was becoming a disc jockey (DJ) on the campus radio station. I love music and thought being a radio DJ would be a great release from college studies. You may foolishly believe DJ'ing is for extroverts. If so, it's likely that you've never been inside a college radio station transmission room. You sit all alone for two- to four-hour shifts and play music. There is a vague sense of others listening to the music remotely, but you exist in your own little universe, a small booth of music, for an extended period of time. You have plenty of time during the songs to plan on-air patter between sets, and you are only speaking into a microphone. For an introvert who also derives energy from music, this was a haven. Even when I carried the weight of the world—or at least the weight of the campus library—in with me, I always left revitalized.

The natural progression from the station booth for college DJs is the frat party. Isn't this taking the well-adjusted introvert thing a bit far? Isn't a frat party the ultimate extrovert mosh pit? Well, yes. That's why I never went to frat parties. Except as the DJ. It's true that DJs are central to a party, but take a closer look. The DJ has a clear place and a specific role. DJs need not make small talk or talk at all, wearing headphones most of the time. Song requests are in writing. You are comfortably alone at a party, in charge of the music; you get to people watch; and—this is the amazing part for a student—you are paid to be there! It's a pretty swank college job. You get free drinks. Plus, it is a surefire conversation starter for years to come.

Compare being a DJ with other roles at a party—like bartending. This person also has a clearly defined role and position—and is expected to make continuous small talk, with no time alone. See the difference?

DJ'ing a party may not top the standard list of introvert-friendly situations, yet it includes many comforting factors for me—time alone, a clear role and position, making people happy, and fantastic music. These are all components of live DJ work.

Remember to think outside the box for introvert-friendly opportunities.

CHAPTER NINE

the job search

It is so simple to be wise. Think of something stupid to say, and don't say it.

—Sam Levenson

Role Reversal Quiz

When do introverts and centroverts talk a blue streak in job interviews?

Answer:

When they are underprepared.

You're on Candid Camera

What a great show. I'm not a big television watcher, but I'd love a revival. The original reality TV. Here is the deal. You *are* on candid camera. Not to encourage delusions of grandeur or freak you out with visions of Big Brother, but Orwell was onto something. More often than you may realize, someone or other is observing your behavior.

Recall a time when you observed a total stranger engaged in a single situation and you extrapolated a whole set of values based on a one-minute event. Perhaps it was at an airport, in an elevator, or observing a stranger talking on a cell phone.

You saw a person in action. Your inner monologue kicked into high gear, and you brilliantly summed up that stranger's whole persona in less time than it took you to go through airport security.

Because of how our brains function, we are hardwired to categorize. That means when observing new people we collect and conclude data. *Hmmm . . . she is taking a lot of notes; she must be a sharp cookie. Or his briefcase is spilling out everywhere; he is a mess. She is talking too loudly on her cell phone; she is disrespectful. He is checking out his reflection in the window—must be vain.*

I've got news for you, sugarplum. You aren't the only one jumping to conclusions as if attending the bungee-cord world championships.

Particularly when on a job search, remember your appearance. Those of us with inner-directed natures may be less focused on external appearances than the average extrovert. An introvert may profess not to care about something as externally driven as looks; this can lead to a somewhat disheveled appearance.

My advice to clients (by holding this book you became a lucky, cut-rate client): be aware of what you can control and what you cannot.

Make a conscious effort to put the best version of yourself out there. And cut others some slack when making your own observations.

The best, most versatile networking technique is—a smile. Why, you ask skeptically, is smiling my number one networking tool? Hear me out on this.

1. It is nonverbal. Translation: Requires *no talking!* Woo-hoo!
2. It offsets the network sand-trap of being labeled standoffish.
3. It is a secure move. People who smile are perceived as confident.
4. Smiling is an invitation for others to approach you in conversation.
5. It makes you happy. Scientific experiments have shown this is true—emotions follow actions.

Malcolm Gladwell's brilliant book *Blink: The Power of Thinking Without Thinking* (Little, Brown and Co., 2005) presents scientific studies that demonstrate "Emotion can . . . start on the face." Gladwell explains that the act of smiling triggers a positive mood rather than only the other way around.

Perhaps you are thinking:

- *I am not the smiley type.*
- *I can't smile if it's not real.*

Thanks for leveling with me. I understand. However, I have learned that the conscious act of plastering a smile on my face before entering a room has a higher payback and lower cost than any other accessory under the sun.

Think of something funny and make it real. Snap to it.

Complainers never prosper.

Are You Really Underconnected?

Social networking is the widely adopted term for online communities and connections. A rather incongruent description, as there is nothing traditionally social about communicating *en masse* with large numbers of widely scattered, separated people.

Social networking devices such as LinkedIn, Facebook, and Twitter carry different associations, value, and meaning to introverts and extroverts. Many extroverts grow visibly excited by the prospect of new ways to expand their network to unprecedented size and scope. Most introverts I know think of on-line networking more as an increasingly necessary nuisance to put on their to-do list.

I know strong extroverts who pride themselves on hitting the five-hundred-plus mark. I know highly successful, savvy introverts who remain at a surprisingly steady five years behind the times on any new social network developments.

Super-connector typically refers to those with an extraordinary amount of connections, generally in the realm of social networking. On this playing field, extroverts leap to the forefront.

Extroverts display networking finesse through their extreme numbers of contacts, wide circles of business associates and online professional networks.

Introvert networkers, on the other hand, strive for depth. This means fewer, stronger connections. It is not possible for an introvert to refer to hundreds of people as friends. That is a carefully guarded term reserved for the select few.

Relationship maintenance is also more demanding for introverts—due in part to the fact that relationships are more draining for introverts, and also because introverts define relationships differently—more depth, more customization, and more effort. Similarly, introverts are unlikely to send out preprinted holiday letters; they are more inclined to write individual cards to fewer recipients.

Will the real super-connector please stand up? Is it the person with loads of electronic friends, effortlessly updated with a single click of the *Send* button, or the one with a few dozen colleagues invested with several years of rapport, trust, and shared experiences?

To answer, start by deconstructing the phrase super-connector. Does "super" necessarily imply high volume? Or can it mean doing something exceptionally well? Unless one has infinite time available, a greater quantity inevitably means a relatively decreased depth of connection.

Super [as prefix]: over and above; higher in quantity, quality, or degree.

Connect: 1. to become joined. 2. to have or establish a rapport.

—Oxford English Dictionary

There is no single answer. The prefix super- could reference higher quantity *or* quality. The verb *connect* can mean simply joining (as in a club, association or community) *or* establishing lasting rapport. Your response to the question depends upon whether you believe quality or depth of connections merits the prefix super-.

Therefore, whether or not you label yourself—or others—as underconnected depends on which part of the definition you emulate. Going for quality and rapport is not so shabby. You have my permission to replace the prefix under- with super-, even with a small, committed network.

 Pause

A flurry of research on how long it takes to undo first impressions resulted in the following range: "eight more meetings" to "nearly impossible" to "you can't." Therefore the definitive answer is between eight and infinity meetings.

The number I was taught in business school is two hundred—it takes about two hundred times the amount of information to undo a first impression than it takes to make it. That is a pretty big number, in case you didn't notice. Let's go with this until we're proven wrong. So although it may take me an instant to impress on you the type of person I am, if you decide I'm rude or dull or insecure or lazy, I have to work two hundred times as hard to disprove your belief as it took for me to make it. So *especially* if you are lazy (can we call you efficient?), be certain to make a good first impression!

Notes From the Field
Just Desserts

In some networking seminars, I start by telling participants to pair up with someone in the room they do not know. Ideally someone they've never even seen before. With writing utensils and paper in hand, they pair off, avoiding conversation prior to instructions.

I tell the pairs they have a total of sixty seconds to talk to each other about their favorite desserts. Go! At thirty seconds I instruct them to switch who is talking. Then I halt the dialogues and ask them to write three words or phrases that describe their partner, based on these brief interactions. Whatever comes to mind first, based on their intuition. I show a list of descriptors (curious, spontaneous, decisive, spunky, concise . . .), but they can write any words that come to mind. This works with groups from ten to over five hundred. Then I ask them to share with each other the three words selected and give each other a reality check—let each know how the other did.

At this point I call for a show of hands for how many people think their partners did a pretty good job of finding three words to describe them. Virtually every hand in the room is raised.

A remarkable component of this activity is that among tens of thousands of participants in my programs, from all industries, functions, and walks of life, not once has anyone ever refused to select three words to describe a complete stranger after listening to this person describe a favorite dessert for thirty seconds! Never. Every single person has dutifully written down three words based on this very limited data. And virtually every hand goes up. This says quite a bit about how people form first impressions—and their general accuracy. Important networking lessons unfold:

1. People form first impressions lightning fast.
2. Often people are right.
3. We want to be right—and will fight for that right.
4. We need to control what we can and manage what we cannot.

We pick up on cues that help us categorize behavior styles unconsciously and generalize patterns. When the partner says, "I don't know, there are so many delicious desserts!" we recognize that the person may not be terribly decisive. When another describes the way the frosting looks, we realize he is precise. When a third gets teary reminiscing about a favorite aunt's apple pie, we understand she is sentimental—or a very big pie fan.

Participants consistently reach consensus that we make first impressions fast and do not even need to hear someone speak to form those impressions. Dessert conversations are just . . . icing on the cake.

The flip side is the *halo effect*. If I like one thing about you—say, your friendly smile—my subconscious transfers and expands this information. You develop a lovely little invisible halo over your head as I determine that I like everything about you! I conclude that you are bright, a good team player, kind, thoughtful, funny, and dedicated. There is a big payoff for a positive first impression.

Take Action!
"Modeling Positive Impressions"

Think of a person who made a lasting, positive impression when you first met. Your example can be from any context of your life—personal or professional, recent or long ago. Generally the first person to come to mind is the best example; don't edit your initial response.

A person who made a positive, lasting first impression on me: _____. If it's a long name, abbreviate. There's no time to waste.

What qualities and traits did this person exhibit?

1. _____

2. _____

3. _____

4. _____

5. _____

What attributes can you authentically model (adapt to make your own) when meeting people?

1. _____

2. _____

3. _____

Some things we admire are difficult to emulate, such as speaking four languages. Others can be transferred more easily into our own repertoire, such as focusing on others when talking. Circle the attribute you want to develop first, starting today.

 Process

For introverts and centroverts, self-promotion while searching for a new job can be a daunting prospect. No worries.

All you need to do is use your natural strengths. Think before you talk (pause), write and practice a very short "advertisement" about yourself (process), and have your mini-speech ready-to-go when needed (pace).

Perhaps you have attended hard-core networking events with an open microphone. Attendees each get thirty seconds to tell everyone else about themselves. Although the opportunity makes some people blanch just thinking about it, the concept is solid.

The question is—what would you say? And what about the more typical situations when people ask about you? Are you prepared? If not, you are prohibited from moving forward before completing this exercise. You will thank me later.

Meet the *thirty-second elevator pitch*. My clients regularly share awe-inspiring stories about the impact of honing these little gems. Perhaps you have heard of the sixty-second speech. That will not do. Less is more. Brevity is more challenging and effective than a ramble. You know this from memories of being on the receiving end.

Most people do not bother to take the time to create an advertisement for themselves. That is downright irresponsible. Not to mention foolish and shortsighted. You certainly do not belong in that category.

The term *elevator pitch* has its origins in the following hypothetical scenario—you find yourself on an elevator with a person of influence. To your surprise, she turns to you and says, "Tell me about yourself." This ride is your first and perhaps only opportunity to have her full attention. What happens?

I have heard several real-life versions similar to the situation just described. Once a senior executive in the U.S. government regaled a group of rising stars with his experience of thirty years earlier, when he actually found himself in an elevator with the head of his department. He was impressively prepared for this chance occurrence, because that's the type of guy he is. The "elevator executive" became his mentor as a result of that short ride, accelerating and directing his career from that point forward.

Sound worth it?

A well-designed pitch is succinct and flexible, enabling you to adapt easily to diverse situations. I am here to help.

Take Action!
"Thirty Seconds of Me"

Grab a pen, a scratch pad, and your thinking cap. Here we go.

What is the outcome you want from a successful elevator pitch? This is critical; goals direct your focus.

You may have a few versions of the speech, depending on the venue, listener, and desired outcome. We are using the term *speech* in the loosest possible terms, as it is only thirty seconds and lacks the formality of most speeches. It is helpful to be familiar with the content of your speech while keeping it adaptable for various situations.

In what type of situation are you most likely to use your elevator pitch? At work, networking events, business trips, interviews, educational settings, cold calling? Make this setting the anticipated backdrop for your speech.

Most likely situation: _____

_____

Second most likely situation: _____

_____

How will you use your speech? To find a job, grow your business, identify a mentor, build a professional network, find collaborators?

Primary use: _____

_____

Secondary use: _____

_____

Even seemingly obvious components of your pitch are not. For example, you might think *What is more straightforward than my name?* But even how you introduce yourself can benefit from some forethought.

Do you prefer to be addressed formally or informally? Do you use your middle name, initials, nickname, or abbreviated version of a longer name?

What do you do? The perennial getting-to-know-you question. Again, your response is telling. I run a consulting firm and generally describe myself as a consultant and coach. I go into detail only if asked. I once heard a colleague introduce herself as "a business owner," indicating she identifies more with the fact of owning a business than the content of the work product.

What do you do? _____

_____

What do you want to do? _____

_____

What accomplishments make you most proud?

1. _____

2. _____

What sets you apart?_____

_____

What inspires you about your work?_____

_____

Okay. Enough background work for now. Review what you've written. Put the top components together in a statement of up to ten sentences:

_____

_____

_____

_____

_____

_____

_____

_____

_____

_____

From my experience coaching people on these little gems, most of us lead with a dull opening. Don't do this! You want pizzazz early in your speech. Captivate the listener with what you love about your work or a short anecdote. Talking about what gets you revved up adds oomph. Passion is contagious. When I coach clients, it is fascinating to witness an observable difference in the speaker's energy level when they are telling a vibrant story as opposed to reciting hum-drum statistics.

These speeches are not intended to say everything there is to know about you. They are teasers. They really are mini-advertisements of yourself. A strong pitch leaves your new acquaintance wanting to learn more. This realization frees you from the constraints of trying to cover the breadth of your profession in one fell swoop. Be intriguing, not comprehensive.

Listeners gather two kinds of information. One is the data: "I was graduated from a prestigious institution with a dream degree. I was promoted five times in two years." Far more compelling is the discovery of your personality. This includes physical presence, sincerity, and attitude. Most listeners are not aware that they're soaking in information through these less overt indicators. Yet these components form most of the basis for the listener's decision whether to continue the conversation—and the potential relationship.

Practice first in front of a mirror, then with someone whose opinion you value. Time yourself! Zero in on what works best. If you are up to it, repeat the exercise with a secondary scenario and goal.

Notes From the Field
Calibration

In a job search, rapport is key. One important aspect of building rapport is syncing your communication to complement, rather than clash with, others. A story of failed calibration illustrates the point.

I was taking a connecting flight home from a business trip which became a delayed layover in Oklahoma City. After two hours of waiting, and hearing continually pushed-back flight status reports, it was nearing 10:00 P.M. Finally we were told our flight was cancelled. This tardy announcement was bad news, as there would be no way out until morning. A lengthy line of disgruntled, exhausted would-be passengers wove through an otherwise deserted airport terminal.

No one was happy. In bounded a terribly perky customer service representative, all smiles. Her demeanor would have made her a perfect fit for the Disney World Main Street parade.

We were a long, long way from Disney World. Her mood was so hopelessly incongruent with the customer base that even the meekest in the crowd became nearly ballistic. The indignity! How dare she be in a good mood when our night was ruined! Ruined!

Syncing your tone is called *calibration*. Meet people more or less where they are. This does not mean yelling and screaming to show your support for someone else who is upset. However, an overly relaxed response can be taken as disinterest or even mockery. Acknowledge that you understand why the situation would make someone upset. A display of empathy does not imply that you would react the same way. You are merely validating, rather than discarding the other person's emotional response.

Positive moods are contagious. *Most* of the time. Just as important as being friendly, however, is matching the prevalent energy of the group. If everyone just came out of a session on the dire consequences we face from unchecked global warming, restrain yourself from commenting brightly on what an unexpectedly gorgeous day it is for January.

So when meeting others with the hope of building connections—whether for a potential job opportunity or another networking goal—notice their mood, tone, volume, and speech style. Practice modifications of your baseline style for maximum flexibility.

For example, I have occasionally been accused of being a bit of a loudmouth (another introvert stereotype bites the dust!). Yet I am usually savvy enough to take it down a notch when meeting with a soft-spoken client. My personality is intact; only the outward expression is fine-tuned for purposes of rapport.

 ## Pace

Prioritize your search. To succeed, know your limits. Don't feel compelled to schedule a week chock-full of professional networking events. Try one a week and gauge your effectiveness, inner response, and ability to follow up. Play around with the type, size, and frequency of events to know how to schedule your time and what type of events to target.

 ## Take Action!
"The Job Grid"

Networking can morph into a nebulous, unformulated task. If amoeba impressions are not your thing, try adapting *The Job Grid* chart for your networking needs. An insta-structure for growing your infrastructure. How about that?

This networking grid works as follows. You can enter up to five names in each of the four boxes. *Box A* is for individuals you have met with whom there seems to be mutual interest. The action item here is to pursue the relationship far enough to determine whether there is a mutually desirable fit for a job opportunity.

Box B is reserved for those folks who have demonstrated *they* would like an ongoing connection, but *you* are not yet convinced of the benefit or your own interest.

You have a concerted interest in the people of *Box C*, but they do not seem to be aware of you at this point.

Box D is for names given to you by others or people you know of through the grapevine. You either have not met them directly or don't know them well enough to know your standing.

Me ▶	I'm Interested	Not Sure
Them ▼	**A.** 1) 2) 3) 4) 5)	**B.** 1) 2) 3) 4) 5)
Demonstrated Interest		
Not on Their Radar	**C.** 1) 2) 3) 4) 5)	**D.** 1) 2) 3) 4) 5)

An active, organized networker has people in all four boxes at any given time.

Caution: Exceeding the numbered spaces provided will entangle you in too many loops.

CHAPTER TEN

business travel

You leave something of yourself at every meeting with another person.

—Fred Rogers

On-the-Road Quiz

a. Why does an extrovert join you for dinner on a business trip?

b. Why does an introvert join you for dinner?

Answer:

a. To unwind and enjoy a meal after a long day.

b. To avoid seeming rude.

Pause

Let's talk about your next seatmate on a transcontinental flight. "Whoa!" I can hear you shout all the way from here. "I don't want a conversation on an airplane!" (Introverts can be irrefutably loud when harboring a strong opinion.)

And you wonder why you are underconnected.

I bet introverts account for 75 percent of the sales of those giant, circa-1970s noise-canceling headphones. That's right; introverts pop them right over their ears to dissuade any hope of conversation from fellow passengers.

Take off those headphones for a minute, I'm talking to you!

Let's make a deal. You can ignore your seatmates for at least 90 percent of the flight. I ask for only about 10 percent of your time. Doesn't that sound more than reasonable?

I fly a lot. I am always flying to or from an event where I am expected to talk. At times I am in a perpetual state of dipping into energy reserves and feeling wiped out. I understand not wanting to talk. Yet I have made some wonderful contacts on airplanes, pain-free.

My best airplane story unfolded when I was sitting there, safely buckled in, reviewing speaker evaluations from a conference, happily ignoring my fellow passengers. The feedback was glowing, along the lines of "Devora is the best consultant I've ever encountered," and "I will only attend events Devora is running from this point forward."

Suddenly my row mate interrupted my reverie (the nerve!), asking, "Are you a consultant?" Clueless as ever, I replied, "How do you know?!" He admitted peeking at my feedback forms, so I held up the heap, saying, "Here, take 'em!" Turned out he was the newly minted VP of professional development for the northeast region of a large corporation. He skimmed the evals, took my card, and the rest is history. (Yes, we still do business.) In that situation I really didn't have to do anything. Usually a bit more initiative is required.

Notes From the Field
Introverts, Travel, and Email

The more business travel one does, the more dependent one becomes upon email and texting to communicate with the home office.

Do introverts and email mix? It is a love-hate thing.

An introverted executive coaching client of mine claimed to be adamantly anti-technology yet eventually confessed "I love email." He explained, "It gives me a chance to think over my responses, to refine what I say before saying it, and avoid conversing with others when I'm worn out."

That is the love part. The flip side is the propensity to overly scrutinize email, attributing unintended meaning. We also miss out on the marvelous information and rapport that can be gained only in direct human interaction.

In a perplexing, poignant dichotomy, introverts seem to have a co-dependent relationship with email. (If any therapists are reading this, I am sure to get an earful about my cavalier use of psychological terms. Sorry.) We are magnetically drawn to the concept of, as one introvert put it "having a conversation without having a conversation."

Plane and train rides home are ideal opportunities to dash off a series of quick lovely-to-meet-you emails while conversations are still fresh in your mind. Driving yourself back, not so much.

LESSON ONE

You NEVER know who is sitting next to you.

I learned this the hard way, in a story that reveals me in a less than stellar light. As a Cornell MBA student flying from Ithaca, NY to Manhattan for an Important Job Interview, I was seated next to a stately gray-haired man who was marking edits on papers. I ignored him because I was engrossed in reviewing materials on the company that was flying me out (still a novelty in those days). He initiated a conversation. I was not interested, but inquired politely, "What are you working on?" He responded, "Writing a book." I smiled indulgently, said, "Well, good luck," and turned back to my reading.

Upon landing, I marched off the airplane and into the taxi I was sharing with four other MBAs from my class (we weren't important enough to merit solo cab rides quite yet). They tumbled in, beside themselves. "We can't believe it! You have all the luck! How come these things only happen to you??"

I had no idea what they were talking about. Turns out everyone except me on the flight recognized my seatmate as the Dean of Cornell University, a major figure in the academic community and a well-respected businessman. He also had a reputation for taking students under his wing. I had completely blown an opportunity thrown at me! Don't let this happen to you.

The epilogue: I no longer have the faintest clue what company or job I was interviewing for on that trip. I believe I did not receive an offer. The only figment of memory left, etched permanently, is of me gallantly dissing the Dean.

Anyone you encounter could transform from a complete stranger into a major player in your life. It happens. Isn't that possibility worth a few minutes of your time?

No need to converse through the whole flight. Be pleasant and casually greet anyone already seated in your row as you situate yourself. I bring gum for takeoff and landing, and I always offer my row-mates a stick. It doesn't matter whether they say yes or no; it is a lovely and appropriate gesture. Other openers, depending on the location of your seat:

- Do you prefer the window shade open or closed?
- Do you want this [newspaper/magazine]?
- Want me to get the light for you?

Then I turn to my work or book. When the drink or snack order is taken, that's round two. I am pleasant and may make a remark or two. If they are enthusiastically responding, I generally let it go on for a few minutes, then sigh and select from the following:

- Unfortunately, I have tons of work to do!
- I'm going to go back to my book now, excuse me.
- I really need a nap before landing.
- It's been nice talking with you!

Be firm and friendly. A short sentence to let them know it's not about them.

From time to time, you will find yourself sincerely wanting the conversation to continue—because you believe there is real potential for a continued relationship or you just sense a spontaneous connection. In either case, as long as you perceive mutual interest, enjoy the conversation. Then follow up with a friendly email or text within twenty-four hours.

Prepare yourself for the occasional challenge. Recently I offered an extrovert my newspaper, only to be subjected to a play-by-play of his hectic travel and travails over the past four months. (I never said this was going to be easy.) I mustered an empathetic smile, congratulated him on his tenacity, and moved on to my selection from the previous four all-purpose bullets. He promptly turned to the person across the aisle for a seamless conversation substitute.

Upon descent, if you have interest in further networking, re-emerge to offer your card and wish your new connection well. It goes without saying you *always* have your cards everywhere you go. There is limited time remaining to converse and the flight concludes on a friendly note. Ta-dah! A formula for flying.

Process

Business trips can be tough. Introverts need alone time—a challenge on many trips, conventions, meetings, and retreats. What is an introvert to do?

There can be significant internal and external pressure to socialize and network—a delicate balancing act. Although travel presents an opportunity to get to know others in a unique environment, too much of that can run an introvert into the ground.

Prior to your trip or at least en route, create your agenda and make a list of potential networking opportunities, such as meals, programs, or free time. Review this list of options and slash it in half. Now half of your open time is designated for you and half for others. Unscheduled spontaneous social time is not ideal for most introverts. Instead, plan in advance when, where, with whom, and for what you will connect with others. If there is a welcome reception, plan to go with one other person you know, if possible. It takes the edge off.

Notes From the Field
It's Just Lunch!

During my programs, clients frequently have lunch together. I usually mumble something about having work to do and graciously (or so I like to believe) bow out of the communal meal. Once, on an evaluation form under Areas for Improvement, a participant wrote "Devora should eat with us." This comment caught my attention.

Everything is a trade-off. In my case, the best scenario is when I teach I/E prior to lunch, so participants just laugh and wave on their way out the door, saying, "We would invite you to eat with us, but we know you need to energize!"

Keep it short. Less is more! Repeat after me:

"Thanks, but I am going to take it easy tonight."

No elaborate explanation or apology required, allowing others to poke holes in your reasoning, unlike this one:

"I need my sleep." → **"You can sleep on the airplane tomorrow!" or**
"I am sure we will be back by 10!"

This discussion is not worth your energy; it's an energy drain itself.

Perhaps you are thinking, *Devora has never met the persistent, off-the-chart extroverts I know!* Well, take a look at two sample dialogues. Do you recognize how good intentions turn into peer pressure and guilt trips? The extrovert is the same in both; only the introvert's responses change.

BAD

E: Hey, you're joining us tonight, right? Everyone is meeting in the lobby at 6:30 p.m.

I: Ummmm . . . [hasn't prepared a response, trying to drum one up last minute]

E: Great! It's going to be a blast—first drinks, then dinner at a terrific steakhouse.

I: Ahhhh, actually, I'm kinda wiped out from today.

E: You have over an hour to rest up! Let's meet at the bar at 6:00, before the others.

I: Well, maybe.

E: Don't be a deadbeat! Everyone is going.

I: I think I'm going to take it easy tonight.

E: But you just said yes. We never see you out. People will start to talk!

I: Okay. [dreading the night and kicking himself]

E: Hey, you're joining us tonight, right? Everyone is meeting in the lobby at 6:30 p.m.

I: I don't think so.

E: Don't be a deadbeat! Everyone is going. Come on, it'll be fun!

I: Thanks; I'm going to take it easy tonight.

E: What?? We never see you out. People will start to talk, ha-ha!

I: I'm going to take it easy tonight. Have fun. See you tomorrow!

REFRAME

Reframe the idea that you are rejecting the group. Remind yourself that it's great the extroverts are making the most of their trip. Just like them, you are making the most of your trip.

How protective you are of your *I-time* depends on your current energy level and your placement on the introvert continuum. A strong introvert running on energy reserves requires more solo time between meetings. A slight introvert with stored energy may join up with the others yet turn in early. If the latter is your action plan, prepare a way to return to the hotel on your own and depart without feeling guilty or self-conscious.

 Pace

Make a list of potential networking opportunities. Mark with a star those that most appeal to you personally. I attended a large conference that was four days of pure networking. I prioritized events and took frequent little breaks. The conference was in Washington, D.C., and one evening's festivity was at the National Air and Space Museum. I chose that as my single evening event to attend because it sounded interesting—plus I knew I could wander the exhibits if I needed time alone. Because I was not worn out from going to every social event offered, I had a great time and met terrific contacts.

When you are interested, you are interesting.

When you are energized and engaged, you are at your networking best.

THE CASE OF THE RAMBLING INTROVERT

When an introvert discovers a connection with another person, his instinct is to stick around. Particularly if it is early in the event, after about ten minutes, offer your companion an out. Remember, she is also here to meet others and may not want to be trapped in one conversation too long, however pleasant the exchange.

You want to leave her with a positive impression of the interaction, prior to running out of things to talk about and the introduction of awkward pauses. Graciously offer an exit: "Do you want to get back to meeting others? I'd enjoy continuing our conversation another time." You need to get back out there too, and now you are buoyed by an early networking victory.

Take Action!
"Making Conversation"

You meet an extrovert who immediately begins telling you all about herself. Much of the information is what you would consider personal, yet you realize this is from your subjective introvert lens. Do you:

A. Listen well and ask good questions until it is time to part ways?
   or
B. Offer up some of your own personal life, even though it feels awkward?

Without proper preparation, you would face only these two options. Being true to your nature, the acceptable choice is A. Yet a one-way relationship is not sustainable or much fun for either involved.

Fortunately you, in your infinite wisdom, are reading this book. Together we can prepare a third, vastly superior alternative. This reminds me of when I brought in a nearly failed accounting exam to my MBA professor, who after patiently reviewing every question said brightly, "I bet between the two of us we would have gotten an A!" But never mind that.

Preparation suits introverts because we think to talk. Advance planning transforms an off-putting situation into a comfortable one.

1. Prepare a list of useful professional facts about yourself.
2. Prepare a list of personal facts you are willing to divulge.

Ensure that your facts have these attributes:

- Short
- Positive
- Versatile
- Easy to explain
- Interesting without bragging
- Opportunities to discover mutual connection

To jump-start the process, write examples for the following:

Professional Data

- Current job and workplace . . .

_____

- What inspires me about my job . . .

_____

- A professional accomplishment . . .

_____

- An interesting early or past job ...

  _____

- A favorite quote ...

  _____

- A professional goal ...

  _____

Personal Tidbits

- Hobbies and interests ...

  _____

- I am from ...

  _____

- I am proud of ...

  _____

- A recent or favorite vacation ...

  _____

- A family fact ...

  _____

- A personal goal ...

  _____

Test-drive your responses aloud with a trusted colleague, friend, or family member. Doing so serves two purposes. You commit your options to memory, making them quickly accessible when caught in the moment. Also, your listener can help you weave these comments seamlessly into a conversation—preventing disjointed non-sequiturs.

Some can be adapted into openers:

> "My daughter would love this place!"
> "This is so different from Boston."
> "I just took a great walk outside—perfect weather."

"I started my own garden and aspire to grow peppers like these."

"This program is well done. Running a conference is tough!"

Or ask questions:

"What do you know about the keynote speaker tomorrow?"

"Do you live far from here?"

"When did you arrive?"

"Do you have any tips about things to do here?"

"How long have you worked in this field?"

"Have you been to this conference before?"

. . . the list goes on. Practice makes inventing new questions easier.

Make comments affirming, not an opportunity to complain. Critical remarks get tossed around with astonishing regularity and reveal a lot about a personality.

- This isn't a very inspired food selection.
- Couldn't they have provided group transportation?
- These nametags sure don't stay on well.
- Seems like they skimped this year.
- I hate these events.
- Isn't the speaker ever going to stop talking?
- I can't stand this city.
- What terrible weather!
- I'm exhausted.
- Look at these drink lines.
- This hotel has gone downhill.

Can you tell I've attended many conferences and am a professional eavesdropper? This list flows out all too easily and could fill a book. Not a particularly inspiring book, yet lengthy. I have heard all of the above, and then some, at networking events. Do you want to hang out with the people who made these comments? Me neither. Don't be one of them.

An introvert with a plan can make a well thought out small-talk strategy seem off-the-cuff. Carefully worded questions can gently open the door for further conversation.

I do not recommend asking a new acquaintance about his or her family. Family is a touchy topic for many and can lead to an awkward interaction. However, stating "My daughter would love this place" opens the door for connectivity where appropriate. Examples of potential responses to such an opening:

- How old is she?
- Do you have a photo with you?
- I have a daughter too . . .
- I have sons, and they would wreck the place!

All of these provide different platforms for connection.

Take Action!
"As If"

Welcome to the world filled with *as if reframes*. So glad to have you join us on this tour of new and improved reality interpretation.

Here's how it works. Write down any operating belief. Virtually *anything* works. If you have no idea what I'm talking about, humor me and jot down a fact—remotely related to networking—that you believe to be true. If you are feeling noncommittal, here are some examples:

- I can't network.
- People don't like me.
- If I act friendly I won't be authentic.
- I am not capable of being more assertive.
- Sheila is not interested in what I have to say.

What if you behaved *as if* your belief weren't true? This has nothing to do with objective reality—which is handy, because reality does not really exist. (Remind me to cover that in this book's sequel.) The *as if frame* challenges you to live *as if* something different were true. Just for kicks, let us practice by replacing the preceding list of beliefs with options from the following selection. Go ahead, check off your favorites. Remember, reframing requires a leap of faith, or for you logical folks, perhaps a suspension of disbelief—this is not about knowing for certain whether or not something is empirical fact. The point is rewiring your brain for heightened success, not winning a debate tournament.

How would your behavior change if you behaved *as if* the following were true?

- I can network.
- People like me.
- I can be friendly and true to myself.
- I can be more assertive in meeting people.
- I am interested in what Sheila has to say.
- Sheila is interested in what I have to say.
- I am interested in what I have to say.

Want another handy application of this little tool? Think back on the last time you went to a social or professional event and got stuck for a period of time talking to the *wrong person*. I think you know what I mean. Someone who you, in your infallible insta-wisdom, determined could be of no use to you whatsoever. You may protest that you do not think of others so callously. Okay, even if you did not have such a harsh thought, perhaps this inner monologue excerpt rings a bell:

Why did I bother coming out tonight? Now I am stuck talking to this stick-in-the-mud. I mean, really. I am so annoyed. I got cornered, and now this is turning into a complete waste of time. (Yawn.) Maybe if I look around the room long enough, he will pick up on my cues and move on. Not with my luck. How can I get out of here gracefully?

What if you were to pretend, for a trial period of three months, that everyone is the right person—if only for the length of time of that particular encounter? What do you imagine would happen? I will make an educated guess, based on the experiences of several hundred clients.

When you choose to believe anyone in front of you is the person who is supposed to be there at the moment, guess what? Due to your innovative approach to meeting people, you treat her like the right person. She temporarily becomes the right person. You become more animated, less distracted, more interested, and more interesting yourself, opening new opportunities for you both.

I am pretty good at reading people, picking up on subtle cues, and noticing personality indicators. Yet I am regularly wrong about who will eventually become the right people in my life. I think this is important to remember. I like that I am wrong, that I cannot always distinguish who will eventually become important in my life story and who will be forgotten fast.

Behave *as if* everyone is the right person. There are infinite variations on *as if* frames. Go crazy! Enjoy! You can practice this tool anytime, anywhere.

In my experience, on-the-road is the ideal time to test-drive new behaviors.

CHAPTER ELEVEN

creating events that work for all

The voyage of discovery consists of seeing the territory with new eyes.

—Marcel Proust

No-Event-Is-a-Good-Event Quiz

True or false:
> Casual events are better than structured activities for people who hate networking.

Answer:

False.

Again and again I have seen the surprising reality unfold—the same people who grumble over structured meet-and-greets benefit, by far, the most.

Let's say you are in charge, running an event to call your own. Well, maybe someone else gets the credit and is thanked from the podium on the big night, but you and I know it was really all your doing. Perhaps it is not officially a networking event, but as we already agreed, everything counts as networking.

How do you create and run an introvert-friendly event? How can you apply your own awareness of personality types to create events sensitive to diverse styles?

Start at the beginning.

 Pause

Stop and think. When planning an event, do you kick off with a brainstorming session? Many do. Your committee might brainstorm ideas for venue, theme, scope, and virtually any other aspect of the program. Yet most brainstorming sessions are inherently extro-centric. Consider the following.

Someone poses a topic, standing at attention in front of the group armed with a giant pen and dry erase board. Suggestions are solicited. Some participants call out ideas, dutifully transcribed for all to see. Others say nothing. To the novice observer, only the active participants are invested in the process, whereas the silent ones are (select one): disinterested, dull, daft, distracted, or desultory. And those are just the d's.

The participants are the extroverts. The process is custom-made for people who talk to think. The whole idea of most brainstorming sessions, really, is to talk until the group agrees on one idea. Introverts respond to the query posed by thinking to talk; however, by the time they have ideas deemed well-formed enough to speak aloud, the typically fast-moving process has progressed to the next logical phase of a brainstorm session (analyzing followed by ranking). An exception to this rule is that introverts speak up—quickly and at length—when a topic of deeper, specific interest to them is broached.

Luckily, there is an easy fix to the terrible injustice done to introverts in brainstorming sessions the world over.

When you are in charge of a brainstorming session for an upcoming event, first tell the group the topic or question at hand. Provide writing instruments and paper. Then ask participants to take a moment to reflect and think over some potential solutions, inviting them to write down their ideas.

One or two minutes is ample. Introverts aren't slow, just thoughtful. Keep track of time; do not trust yourself to guess when the minute is up—it is a proven fact that time flows faster to the person standing up in front of the group than for seated participants.

Notes From the Field
Watch Your Step

Why are lively introverts mislabeled extroverts? Most such judgments are based on imperfect observation.

In my case, I am seen flitting happily around a room chatting with a range of people, bursting with energy. How is this possible? This occurs only because of what is not seen. A closer look reveals that I frequently slip away to recharge. That I focus on one-on-ones, drifting away from group conversation. That I almost never attend evening programming, preferring to turn in early. That during conferences I inhale meals (a habit I do not recommend), dashing out early for extra *I-time*. That in meetings I think through and write down my thoughts before offering contributions. And that when in small groups I process long before making my opinions known.

If I followed extro-centric networking advice I would squelch my natural instincts, forcing myself to socialize as much as possible—with dismal results.

Yet when introverts have a deeper connection with someone—watch out! Those inner layers tear off, unleashed.

Next, invite people to call out ideas and/or pass forward their written ideas, which you can read aloud and add to the visible list. Prepare to be surprised by how many more ideas you get from the entire group.

 Process

Early in the process of event preparation, take time to identify the hidden resources of those around you. Learn a bit about people's interests, backgrounds, and skills. Provide a brief survey, increasing response rate and depth from introverts. Also, share information about the event with those around you, opening the door to new ideas and input. By doing so, you can avoid situations like this next example.

One of my non-profit clients ran a major event highlighting the customs of a distant culture. Only afterward did the event planner learn that the spouse of a colleague was from that culture. She would have been a wonderful resource, yet no one thought to share information about the event throughout the medium-sized agency.

What's the best way to integrate introverts, centroverts, and extroverts at an event? The solution is counterintuitive. Many people assume that introverts do not want to be coerced into interactions. Even introverts themselves claim to dislike any coordinated efforts to engage with unknown others. Don't believe them! I have been down this road many times, and I am here to tell you that introverts benefit from many, organized interactions. Extroverts generally engage with strangers no matter what. It is the introverts (and centroverts) who have a tough time meeting people in unstructured situations. Coordinating methods to open conversation and mix up participants is doing your introverted friends a big favor, believe me.

ASSUME NOTHING

When you're planning events, make no assumptions. As a consultant, I inevitably get an earful about lack of resources—not enough time, money, volunteers, and so on. Yet I notice that the committee makes assumptions about what people will and won't be willing to do or contribute. Big mistake!

A variation on these limiting assumptions occurs when planners think only extreme extroverts will want to participate in structured networking activities. The precise opposite is true. The more a person hates networking, the more that person will grudgingly welcome an activity that creates structured interactions.

 Pace

A networking event that works for all has a pace that flows between structure and open time. Among the dozens of integration activities I know, the samples here are easiest to apply and have the broadest application. Use your judgment and adapt to taste. One or two per event is ample.

PLACE CARDS

My version of place cards works best at small to medium-sized conferences (forty to two hundred participants) with multiple group meals. Make place cards with a range of creative descriptions and put one at each place setting (*speak 3-plus languages, play golf, have a Ph.D., know how to juggle, love to cook, avid reader . . .*) Have extras and blanks on hand. As people enter, invite them to sit at a place with a description that fits. This setup serves a dual purpose. People sit with a mix of others, and each place card is a mini-conversation starter—providing topics to discuss. If a few people cannot find a match, they can pick from the extras or write their own.

NAMETAG ART

Provide multi-colored pens next to the nametags. Ask people to add on the nametag a small drawing that symbolizes something about themselves. As participants circulate in the room, these symbols provide a starting point for mingling, offering greater insight into others than typical introductory conversations. I have tried this with conservative, serious groups, and they loved the results.

ACTION BINGO

A bit of upfront work and creativity pays off with this activity. Create several different versions of bingo boards—make each board with four boxes across and down for a total of sixteen squares. I make about ten versions per event, but four or five is fine. Write a different attribute, hobby, or trait in each box (*gardener, class cutup, love the snow, never tired, born to ride*—a range of specifics, generalities, metaphors, and so on). Print enough copies to give one board to each person along with a pen or pencil. Provide five minutes to play. Participants find someone else with one of the traits on their board and get that person to sign in the box. Participants cannot sign their own board and can solicit only one signature from any one person. You can give a small prize to the winner(s) at the end—whoever has the most spaces filled. This takes little time, energizes the group, and encourages continued discussion through the facts that people gather.

Near the beginning of an informal meet and greet event, grab a microphone and plug in speakers. Get everyone's attention for a brief activity. Tell them you are going to play music (about fifteen seconds per interlude) and they can walk around. When the music stops, participants turn to someone nearby whom they do not yet know, introduce themselves, and tell each other their response to a topic you announce. Allow only about a minute per interaction; keep it moving. Topic samples include:

- What was your first job?
- Describe your dream meal.
- What is a hidden talent you have?
- Where did you spend a recent vacation?
- Tell about something you won.

Within less than ten minutes, everyone has an opportunity to meet five people.

Learn Names

I have heard that the most beautiful word is your own name.

A client told me his impression of a senior colleague: "He is a really good guy," then reflected with a laugh, "… or maybe it is just because he always remembers my name." There is no doubt that learning and using other people's names is a golden key to swing open the gates of rapport.

Some of my seminars start with short participant introductions. Hardly anyone listens to anyone else. Instead, people are preparing and mentally rehearsing what *they* plan to say.

An hour later, I surprise the group by announcing a contest. Whoever knows everyone's name wins a prize. This announcement is greeted with silence broken by nervous laughter. Then typically, one person—usually an introvert—will methodically, assuredly, and without fanfare, rattle off the names of every other person in attendance.

I have witnessed this scenario dozens of times. Extroverts focus on speaking, introverts on listening. Therefore, introverts are more likely to listen deeply—and remember what is said.

Even so, most introverts and extroverts get a failing grade in *The Basics of Name Recollection*. Following are helpful tips, tested and provided by my clients.

1. First, you have to care. This is a tough pill to swallow, because it is an accusation that not remembering names is equivalent with not caring enough. Yet let's be honest. Many people cannot repeat a name mere moments after they hear it. *We are simply not paying attention.* Focus all your attention on the event and person in front of you.

2. Repeat the other person's name up to three times during your first conversation. More is too much.

3. When first introduced, look directly at the other person's eyes while repeating back his or her name.

4. Make associations.
   a. Familiar names: associate the name with another person.
   b. Unfamiliar names: ask the origin.

Auditory	Visual	Kinesthetic
■ Use the name three times in initial conversation.	■ Envision the name written out.	■ Imagine the person engaged in an alliterated activity, (Rick raking, Cathy cooking).
■ Ask how to spell it, then repeat it for confirmation.	■ Make a visual image of the name.	■ Notice the person's physical stance.
■ Clarify the pronunciation.	■ Look at the nametag.	■ Notice the person's mood and demeanor.
■ Connect the name to his or her voice.	■ Link the name to what the person is wearing.	■ Write down the name soon after talking.
■ Recall a song with the name, if possible.	■ Connect the name to the face.	■ If seated in a group, draw a chart with the names.
■ Say the name lyrically in your head.	■ Picture a person you know with the same name.	■ Draw the letters with your finger through the air...after moving away!

5. Write a summary of information gathered shortly after an initial interaction—where you met, what you discussed, and how to follow up.

Use a memory system in sync with your primary processing system —auditory, visual or kinesthetic. If you do not know your favored system, experiment with all three to discover what technique works best for you.

Everyone	Well-Known Names	Less-Recognized Names
▪ Wear a nametag throughout an event.	▪ Ask whether they know another [your name].	▪ Spell your name slowly.
▪ Place the nametag on your upper left chest—where people are most likely to look.	▪ Clarify spelling.	▪ Offer a rhyme or memory tool.
▪ Repeat your name.	▪ Recall someone well-known with the same name.	▪ Reintroduce yourself the first several times you meet.

DO YOUR PART

Assisting others to remember your name is an important corollary to remembering theirs.

Popular, well-known names vary widely by culture, country, and region. Let's just say that if you have a widely recognizable name, you know it. Do you know three or more people with your first name? Those with less recognizable names may know virtually no one with their name and are accustomed to repeating and spelling their name to people they meet.

COGNITIVE DISSONANCE

To refresh your memory of that freshman Psych 101 class you took in your misguided youth for an easy A, I will remind you of cognitive dissonance. This psychological phenomenon captures the human condition of wanting to be right. Let's say I have a theory. I become attached to my hypothesis. If evidence in the outside world contradicts my hypothesis, my brain kicks into high gear to disprove the data and cling to my theory. Brains loyally collect data to support our beliefs, sorting out, ignoring, and disproving contradictory evidence.

Let's drive this home. Think of what population subgroup you secretly believe are the worst drivers out there. Don't tell me! I don't want my own theory clouded by yours. Imagine you are driving on the highway and in a hurry. You are in the left lane in a 55 mph zone. You assess how fast you can go without being pulled over. So you are cruising along at 64 mph when you come up on a car directly in front of you, plodding along at an inconceivably rude 50 mph. In the fast lane! You swing into the right lane to pass, and can't resist a peek into the other car to check your personal bad driver theory. Aha! It is one of them! You *knew* it! You enjoy a smidgeon of self-satisfaction that you were right.

Now, take the same scenario, except that when passing you peek at the driver and it is *not* one of them. In fact, this driver looks very similar to you. Do you trash your theory? Do you think, *Well, that was a good lesson in human nature, I was wrong?* No. You shrug and think, *Hmpf. That's strange.* And you go on your way. It was a non-event. Data discarded.

How does this connect with creating events that work for all? In event management, planners frequently make assumptions about what will or won't resonate with participants—and sort for data that supports their hypothesis. Raising your awareness of the limitations and pitfalls of cognitive dissonance enables you to expand your receptiveness to new and different ideas.

CHAPTER TWELVE

defining outcomes, achieving goals

We cannot see our reflection in running water; it is only in still water that we can see.

—Taoist Proverb

Disintegration-of-Goals Quiz

True or False:
  Most people fail at their goals because they lack the willpower to follow through.

Answer:

False.
This erroneous belief only demoralizes people aspiring to make
positive changes. Most goals fail because they are poorly formed.

Outcome Goals

Of the many versions of goal-setting out there, *Outcome Goals* are the best. I have taught outcome-based goal setting to innumerable clients with consistently positive, measurable results.

I was coaching Carlos, a senior executive in a Fortune 500 company. By all outward appearances he was well-respected and successful. However, he tended to feel on the outskirts and wanted to improve his networking aptitude.

Rather than just saying he would try harder to get himself out there, we created a challenging yet specific plan. First, recognize that challenges—like all else—are subjective. Carlos worked in a different state from where he lived, and he was very committed to his job. Each weekday he arrived at work early, spent the day in his office and at meetings, left to exercise, and went back to his rented apartment. As an introvert who flew home to a good family life on the weekends, he was mostly satisfied with this arrangement.

However, he believed his career would benefit from improving his professional peer network within his large corporation. We decided an achievable stretch goal for Carlos would be to initiate a lunch or coffee break twice a month for three months with different people he didn't know well. We even created a chart for him to check off. I am a big believer in the grown-up version of sticker charts. They've been around so long for a reason. There's something satisfying and visceral about marking off accomplishments in little boxes. I frequently make customized goal charts for my clients. Introverts can keep them in their top drawer rather than up on the bulletin board, away from inquisitive eyes.

Carlos succeeded at his goal and began new habits of reaching out to others in a way comfortable for an introvert—one-on-one.

Carlos could have set a goal to simply network better or more often. However such goals are sure to fail. Why? They are vague and not measurable. Most goals are poorly formed. They are general and not specific, so there is no way to measure success. Outcome goals to the rescue!

First, it never hurts to prepare oneself for achievement by creating a goal based on one's strengths. Take a moment in review . . .

High-performance introverts shine in:

- One-on-one discussion
- Delving into areas of expertise
- Writing and reflection

Introvert strengths include:

- Focusing attention on others
- Strong listening
- Systematic follow-up

High-performance extroverts shine in:

- Group discussion
- Pursing a range of topics
- Interaction and activity

Extrovert strengths include:

- Promoting projects and people
- Ability to engage in conversation
- Creating excitement for new ideas

Centroverts! Decide which set of strengths resonates with you today and go from there.

OUTCOME GOALS

Outcome goals comprise five unique elements that set the path for lasting success.

POSITIVE

State goals in the positive. We can work toward a desired goal but not away from what is undesirable. Every goal can be rewritten from the negative to the positive. For example, *I am going to stop avoiding networking functions* does not work. *I will attend at least two networking events in the next six months* does.

CONTROL

Although even the most introverted among us remain dependent on others for various resources, a well-formed goal is reasonably within your own control. A poorly formed goal requires either changes in others' fundamental personalities, acts of nature, or significant effort from others.

CONTEXT

An outcome goal is of the appropriate size and scope. This means it is written to maximize motivation and effort. A well-formed goal strikes the perfect balance: it is challenging yet achievable. If I believe a goal is impossible, I will not try. If I think a goal is a piece of cake, I also won't put forth any effort. The stretch goal—that I believe is a long shot yet I can potentially imagine completing—is the most compelling.

ECOLOGICAL

This is an unusual and crucial component of a goal statement. Ecological does not necessarily imply good for the environment, although that is a nice bonus! Think of your life as its own ecosystem—which it is. If one aspect of your life is imbalanced, your life becomes out of sync. To be harmonious your goal must complement, not compete with other important components of your life. Synchronize goals with your values and beliefs. This does not merely mean your goal is ethical. Plenty of goals are perfectly ethical yet not sustainable at this particular time and place in a person's life.

MEASURABLE

Think of yourself as a detective. You need specific clues to know whether you accomplish your goals. Think: *What evidence will let me know I succeeded?* Many people mess up on this one, with goals that are vague and therefore doomed to fail. *I am going to meet more people! I will follow up better! I'll go outside my comfort zone! Just do it!* Guess what? You won't. Because how will you know whether or not you did? You won't.

Any goal can be put in specific terms. A vague goal is unattainable; a clear goal is specific. For example, *I will expand my professional network* becomes *I will sign up this week for the annual industry conference in May and make travel arrangements immediately.* Either you do or you don't. It's hard to fake it.

Here is a form for your use. When you've completed it, remember that goals are most effective when shared—even if just with a few select confidants. Telling people about your goal confirms your commitment, develops support, and increases accountability.

Take Action!
"Outcome Goals"

Answering these two questions provides a sturdy foundation for outcome goal development.

What do I want?

How can successful networking contribute to my success?

_____

_____

_____

OUTCOME GOAL COMPONENTS

A. **State the outcome positively**. You can move toward something you want, not away from something you do not want.

My goal is: _____

_____

B. **Ensure that the outcome is within your control**. Outcomes that rely excessively on other people's actions are not well formed.

Do I have the necessary resources to initiate and maintain the outcome?
If not, what support, skills, or materials do I need to obtain?

_____

_____

C. **Put your outcome in context**. The outcome ought to be of appropriate size and scope. Well-stated outcomes are challenging but achievable.

Where, when, and with whom will I achieve my outcome?

_____

_____

D. **Choose an outcome that is ecological**. Align the outcome with your values and beliefs. Consider the consequences of achieving your goal in the context of your professional work and relationships.

What will I need to give up or take on to achieve my outcome?

_____

_____

E. **What is a sensory-based, testable description of my outcome?** Know the "proof" of an achieved outcome. Describe the outcome as specifically as possible.

What evidence will I have that my goal has been obtained? How will a successful outcome look, sound, and feel?

_____

_____

My first step, within one week, is . . .

_____

_____

This last step is the most important. I have heard the observation that our world is filled with many great beginners yet few great enders. Anyone can initiate the pursuit of new habits yet few transform intention into real change.

see ya later, alligator

Carefully observe the way your heart draws you;

and choose that way with all your strength

—Hasidic Proverb

Are-You-STILL-Here? Quiz

Now that you have stuck around to the very end, you:
   a. Are a bit older and wiser than when you began.
   b. Have learned the secret chant to transform introverts into extroverts.
   c. Can apply your innate strengths to jump-start a networking journey.

Answer:

a+c.

Don't just follow advice. Follow your gut. If bits of advice ring true, a light bulb will illuminate over your head. If not, let it go. Stay true to your inner-directed personal field guide.

When do you fade back? When do you light up?

Move Along

A sure way to fail is to pretend to be someone you are not. This sounds obvious, yet is a path many of us attempt in vain. An enormous factor in successful networking is being comfortable with who you are and putting your best self out there.

The creation of lasting, real connections and the discovery of connectivity is the new, improved way to build a strong, lasting network.

UPON REFLECTION

I don't believe it is true that we learn from experience. I don't know about you, but I can do the same dumb thing over and over yet not learn a thing.

Instead, the learning part evolves from *reflecting* on experience. It is through the vehicle of processing and extracting lessons and recognizing patterns through the lens of curiosity—rather than judgment or victimization—that we learn and develop as people. Consider the following presupposition, a basic precept of Neuro-Linguistic Programming (NLP):

There is no such thing as failure, only feedback.

Thinking *I failed* is a copout! It lets you off the hook. Game over, dude. I am not about to let you off so easily. I run a tight ship.

Try this on for size. Reframe your setbacks as signals for change and the opportunity to improve. This method of thinking requires a lot more energy than *I blew it*. Instead, explode your limiting mindset.

What would happen if you replaced the concept of failure with that of opportunity?

危
机

This is the Chinese character for crisis. It is composed of two stacked figures. Wēi, danger, is above and jī, opportunity, is below. As the complete character implies, what initially poses as danger is a cover for opportunity.

Take Action!
"The Point of It All"

I have road-tested this quick exercise on thousands. It's pretty cool. Try it as you read along. Stand up, get that blood flowing. Hold nothing. Shake out. Put one arm straight ahead, index finger pointing directly in front of you.

Now reach that arm as far back behind you as possible, while keeping the rest of your body still facing forward. Peek back and see how far you stretched your arm. Turn your head around to look without moving your arm. Notice what you are pointing to behind you. Shake out. Assume the identical starting location and repeat the exercise, yet this time reach farther. Peek again. Did you point beyond your first try? Remarkably, every person I have engaged in this activity has reached farther the second time. What was the difference between the first time and the second? Only one tiny detail: the imperative to reach farther. Even though the first time I said to reach as far back as possible. This shift in outcome makes no sense! If you were following the instructions, you reached as far as you could the first time! So how is it possible to reach even farther only a moment later?

You tell me.

Acknowledgments

First, I thank Mark Morrow for introducing me to Berrett-Koehler. Mark took me where I needed to go, and there I met some amazing people, starting with Jeevan Sivasubramaniam. I used to wonder how authors got so lucky as to thank their "publisher and friend," and now it is my turn. Except that Jeevan is also my illustrator, confidant, therapist, nemesis, and alter ego. My editor, Steve Piersanti, is a genius, pure and simple. Steve's brilliance, compassion, depth, and insight drove me beyond myself. Plus, he is a mensch.

For their invaluable advice, admonishments, and adjustments, I thank my manuscript reviewers: Christopher Morris, Linda Norton, Douglas Hammer, and Katherine Armstrong (who embodies above and beyond). Jeremy Sullivan worked tirelessly with Jeevan on all zillion versions of the illustrations and plenty else behind the scenes. I am nuts about every single person at my beloved Berrett-Koehler and especially thank Kristen, Katie, and Mike for the extra energy they continually devote with gracious, generous spirits. The BK Authors Co-op welcomed me into their remarkable community faster than I could say "But I energize alone!" I particularly thank my new, dear friend and guide John Kador.

I thank with all my heart James Killian and the late Alan Pike, who taught me how to write and, parenthetically, how to live. Also, Elaine Biech for publishing me again and again in Wiley and encouraging me to fly forward.

Last, and the opposite of least, I am bursting with gratitude for the unflinching, boundless support of my dear friends and family. If I mentioned each of you by name my entire platform as an introvert would, once again, be called into question. If you don't know who you are, I promise to remind you at regular intervals—immediately preceding my request for yet another favor.

About Only Connect Consulting, Inc.

Since 1996, Only Connect Consulting, Inc. (OCC) has successfully enhanced connections within and among over one hundred organizations. OCC provides clients with tools and systems to strengthen effectiveness and morale.

Through assessments, coaching, and interactive seminars, OCC partners with clients to revise leadership practices, develop long-term initiatives, and integrate lasting change.

OCC programs are customized to meet unique needs. Dynamic learning engages participants in simulations, discussions, and applications. Innovative designs enable participants to relate learning points to current challenges.

Areas of expertise include but are not limited to the following:

- Leadership Development
- Introversion and Extroversion
- Change Management
- Personality Assessment
- Time/Stress Management
- Creative Problem Solving
- Decision Making
- Organization Skills
- Public Speaking
- Diversity
- Managing Up
- Conflict Management
- Theatre-Based Simulations

- Networking
- Team Development
- Communication
- Customer Service
- 360-Degree Feedback
- Coaching/Mentoring
- Meeting Management
- Strategic Planning
- Focus Groups
- Influence/Negotiation
- Building Rapport
- Assessments
- Action Planning

OCC clients include the Smithsonian Institution, U.S. Department of Education, SAIC, Global Intellectual Properties Academy, U.S. Patent and Trademark Office, Department of Homeland Security, Cornell University, FEMA, U.S. Office of Personnel Management, Historically Black Colleges and Universities, and Computer Science Corporation.

For additional information and bookings, visit OCC on the web at www.onlyconnectconsulting.com.

index

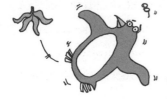 Your Fearless Author

NA'AMA BATYA LEWIN

A resident of Introville, Devora commutes to Extroland for work. After a productive childhood of reading stacks of books and playing games by herself, she received a BA magna cum laude from University of Pennsylvania (Annenberg School of Communication). Putting her degree to good use, she proceeded to freelance as an actress, disc jockey, London chambermaid, tap dancer, hotline counselor, and investigative reporter. In each of these varied endeavors, she strove to keep conversation to a minimum.

After passing Go, she collected an MBA from Cornell University (Johnson Graduate School of Management), where she was a full-tuition merit scholar. She has received a few awards—such as the USDA women-owned business of the year—and is open to winning several more.

Devora is mostly interested in the nuances of personality—and not much else besides food and stuff that sparkles. She loves being a consultant (who knew?) and founded Only Connect Consulting, Inc. (OCC) in 1996. Devora is pleased to have been hired by innumerable top-notch, overwhelmed, underconnected clients. OCC has grown annually on nothing but referrals.

Devora has served as visiting faculty at Cornell University's MBA Leadership Skills Program for fifteen years. As program director of the U.S. Government's prestigious *Presidential Management Fellows Orientation Program*, Devora's design and facilitation received the highest evaluations in the program's history.

Devora teaches leadership, networking, presentation skills, communication, change management, and team development—then retreats to dine alone. Her editors forcibly ordered her to "join" Facebook under much duress.

She is a certified practitioner in Neuro-Linguistic Programming and Myers-Briggs Type Indicator. She is a member of Phi Beta Kappa, American Society for Training and Development, and Mensa.

Devora lives with her supremely patient husband and wildly kinesthetic three sons near Washington, D.C., in what can best be described as a frat house.

THE *ASTD* MISSION:

Through exceptional learning and performance, we create a world that works better.

The American Society for Training & Development provides world-class professional development opportunities, content, networking, and resources for workplace learning and performance professionals.

Dedicated to helping members increase their relevance, enhance their skills, and align learning to business results, ASTD sets the standard for best practices within the profession.

The society is recognized for shaping global discussions on workforce development and providing the tools to demonstrate the impact of learning on the organizational bottom line. ASTD represents the profession's interests to corporate executives, policy makers, academic leaders, small business owners, and consultants through world-class content, convening opportunities, professional development, and awards and recognition.

Resources
- *T+D (Training + Development)* Magazine
- ASTD Press
- Industry Newsletters
- Research and Benchmarking
- Representation to Policy Makers

Networking
- Local Chapters
- Online Communities
- ASTD Connect
- Benchmarking Forum
- Learning Executives Network

Professional Development
- Certificate Programs
- Conferences and Workshops
- Online Learning
- CPLP™ Certification Through the ASTD Certification Institute
- Career Center and Job Bank

Awards and Best Practices
- ASTD BEST Awards
- Excellence in Practice Awards
- E-Learning Courseware Certification (ECC) Through the ASTD Certification Institute

Learn more about ASTD at www.astd.org.
1.800.628.2783 (U.S.) or 1.703.683.8100
customercare@astd.org

080615.31410

Berrett–Koehler
Publishers

Berrett-Koehler is an independent publisher dedicated to an ambitious mission: *Creating a World That Works for All*.

We believe that to truly create a better world, action is needed at all levels—individual, organizational, and societal. At the individual level, our publications help people align their lives with their values and with their aspirations for a better world. At the organizational level, our publications promote progressive leadership and management practices, socially responsible approaches to business, and humane and effective organizations. At the societal level, our publications advance social and economic justice, shared prosperity, sustainability, and new solutions to national and global issues.

A major theme of our publications is "Opening Up New Space." Berrett-Koehler titles challenge conventional thinking, introduce new ideas, and foster positive change. Their common quest is changing the underlying beliefs, mindsets, institutions, and structures that keep generating the same cycles of problems, no matter who our leaders are or what improvement programs we adopt.

We strive to practice what we preach—to operate our publishing company in line with the ideas in our books. At the core of our approach is stewardship, which we define as a deep sense of responsibility to administer the company for the benefit of all of our "stakeholder" groups: authors, customers, employees, investors, service providers, and the communities and environment around us.

We are grateful to the thousands of readers, authors, and other friends of the company who consider themselves to be part of the "BK Community." We hope that you, too, will join us in our mission.

A BK Life Book

This book is part of our BK Life series. BK Life books change people's lives. They help individuals improve their lives in ways that are beneficial for the families, organizations, communities, nations, and world in which they live and work. To find out more, visit **www.bk-life.com**.

Berrett–Koehler
Publishers

A community dedicated to creating
a world that works for all

Visit Our Website: www.bkconnection.com

Read book excerpts, see author videos and Internet movies, read our
authors' blogs, join discussion groups, download book apps, find out about
the BK Affiliate Network, browse subject-area libraries of books, get special
discounts, and more!

Subscribe to Our Free E-Newsletter, the *BK Communiqué*

Be the first to hear about new publications, special discount offers, exclusive articles, news about bestsellers, and more! Get on the list for our free
e-newsletter by going to **www.bkconnection.com**.

Get Quantity Discounts

Berrett-Koehler books are available at quantity discounts for orders of ten or
more copies. Please call us toll-free at (800) 929-2929 or email us at **bkp
.orders@aidcvt.com**.

Join the BK Community

BKcommunity.com is a virtual meeting place where people from around
the world can engage with kindred spirits to create a world that works for
all. BKcommunity.com members may create their own profiles, blog, start
and participate in forums and discussion groups, post photos and videos,
answer surveys, announce and register for upcoming events, and chat with
others online in real time. Please join the conversation!

Mixed Sources
Product group from well-managed
forests, controlled sources and
recycled wood or fiber
www.fsc.org Cert no. SW-COC-003925
© 1996 Forest Stewardship Council
FSC